THE PRIMACY OF LOVE

*An Introduction to the Ethics
of
Thomas Aquinas*

by
PAUL J. WADELL, C.P.

WIPF & STOCK · Eugene, Oregon

Wipf and Stock Publishers
199 W 8th Ave, Suite 3
Eugene, OR 97401

The Primacy of Love
An Introduction to the Ethics of Thomas Aquinas
By Wadell, Paul J.
Copyright©1992 by Wadell, Paul J.
ISBN 13: 978-1-60608-369-7
Publication date 12/16/2008
Previously published by Paulist Press, 1992

Contents

To
My Sisters and Brothers:

Mary, Anne, Amy, Robert, Christine,
Barbara, Thomas, John

Introduction

The purpose of this book is to reintroduce the moral theology of a man who has been picked apart more than any other Catholic theologian. No theologian has been quoted, commented on, and written about more than Thomas Aquinas, but somewhere in the abundance of those pages the spirit of Aquinas may have been lost. Here is a man who was glaringly overweight, had a terrible fear of lightning, and loved God with a passion that cannot fail to inspire.

For a long time I have been convinced that the moral theology of Thomas Aquinas is the hidden treasure of the Catholic moral tradition. It is hidden because it has not been sufficiently appreciated. Too often Aquinas's ethics are presented as being overly rationalistic, excessively formal, and too scholastic to be of use to us today. But that is a disservice to Aquinas and a loss to us all. The core of Thomistic ethics is not the natural law, but the virtues, and the virtues are best understood not as acts of reason, but as strategies of love whereby those devoted to God are transformed in God's goodness. There is nothing heady about this; it is the earthiest and most practical of moralities because it is centered in love, the passion that gives energy and shape to all our behavior.

Too, Aquinas saw no division between the moral and the spiritual life. For him they were one, and to attempt to separate them was to forget that the overall purpose of the moral life was to make us the kind of people whose lives are songs of praise to a God whose love is unending. Thomas knew that the moral life is the Christian life, that to grow in goodness is to be transfigured in holiness, and that charity is no idle love, but is the virtue that makes our whole life an offering to God. The strategy of Thomistic ethics is not primarily to assist us in making good decisions or to help us in resolving problems of conscience; no, its goal is the total transformation of ourselves into people who can call God's Kingdom their home. There is nothing piecemeal or partial about Aquinas's moral theology. Because of the glory it promises, it is the most wholistic and radical ethic imaginable.

1

One does not so much read Thomas's ethics as become part of them. To enter his vision of the moral life is to take up an adventure that will involve us to the center of our being. We cannot study Aquinas and remain untouched. His schema of the moral life will grab us, it will make demands on us, and the longer we travel with him the more we will notice we are not who we were when we began. Surprising changes will take place; we shall be implicated in a conversion. That is why it is important to know the man whose moral theology is not to be read, but lived. Chapter 1 is a brief overview of Aquinas's life. Before we begin our journey, we must know something about who will be leading us. Thomas will guide us into a way of life from which we shall never fully recover. It is fitting that we meet him and learn as much about him as we can. We shall glimpse his struggles, sufferings and frustrations. We will be touched by how generously Thomas put his talents at the service of so many: his Dominican community, the church, and the world. More than anything, we will be moved by the humanity of this man: his humility, his doubts, his dedication, his moments of darkness, but especially his deep, passionate love.

In chapter 2 we enter Aquinas's moral theology. We begin as he did, shaping our account of the moral life by looking first at how human beings behave. Through that observation we learn a simple but important truth: men and women are purposeful. Everything we do bespeaks something we are trying to achieve. We spend time preparing a meal because we want to bring joy to those we love. We work hard on a project because we want to contribute to something bigger than ourselves. We gather in worship because we want to give thanks to a God on whom we absolutely depend. But there is one purpose which embraces them all, one purpose which articulates the desire behind everything we do. This ever-present purpose is our intention for wholeness, completion, happiness and peace. We search for something good that will restore us, we hunger for a love in which we desire no more. For Thomas, morality pivots on desire. It is born from our hunger for something good and perfecting, and it ends when our hearts find peace.

In chapter 3 our investigation continues as we consider how Aquinas understands happiness. He is convinced that happiness is the one thing everybody wants; for him, it is the focus of the moral life. But if this desire for well-being empowers everything we do, it is important that we understand rightly what happiness is. A realist, Aquinas begins his investigation by considering where most people think happiness is to be found. He looks at money, prestige, power and pleasure. And he takes them quite seriously because he knows we cannot have a good life without them. Still, Thomas wants not just something good for us, he wants the best for us, and so he presses on to discover a happiness that does not fail. In possessing what good shall we know the deepest possible joy? It is this question that guides Aquinas's search for where true happiness is to be found.

Not surprisingly, Thomas concludes that our most perfect and enduring joy is found in God. The reason is simple: in God is a goodness money, prestige, power and pleasure lack. As good and as necessary as these things are, they cannot do for us what God can, and God can do infinitely more than we could ever do for ourselves. Thomas sees our happiness in a particular way. For us to be happy is to be related to God in friendship. He calls this friendship charity, and it is the most comprehensive and constitutive activity of our lives. In chapter 4 we shall examine what Thomas means by this. What do we mean when we say our happiness is charity-friendship with God? How can we speak of ourselves as God's friends? We shall look at the marks of friendship, we shall explore what they mean when the friend is God, and we shall discover why, for Thomas, it is through this special relationship that we receive the happiness God has always desired for us.

Aquinas has a love-centered ethic. Our actions are empowered by love because they are born from our desire for something good. Desire is love at work. Through our moral acts we direct our lives to whatever we think will be best for us. Thomas sees it this way. Morality begins in love, works through desire, and is completed in joy. Obviously, then, the passions and affections are integral to Thomas's account of the moral life. In chapter 5 we will look at what Thomas means by the passions, particularly love, and how he sees them empowering moral growth and transformation. As we shall see, far from excising the emotions, Thomas argues that becoming good is a matter of learning to love the right things in the right way.

But that is not always easy. Thomas envisions the moral life as an odyssey through love to the good—but every odyssey is imperiled by adversity, threatened by bad luck. The plot of the moral life is to move through love to the good, and in the good to find joy. This may be easy when life cooperates and everything goes our way, but that is not always the case. Sometimes life does not cooperate and we are upended by misfortune. Sometimes we simply tire of pursuing the good, we grow disenchanted, our original zeal dims. Thomas sees two sets of emotions in the moral life. The first charts the direction of the moral life and captures our position toward the good. In this sense we speak of the moral life beginning in love, continuing through desire, and culminating in joy. But we need another set of passions and emotions to enable us to remain steadfast in our quest for the good and not grow dispirited. Here emotions such as courage, hope and anger become crucial in our odyssey to the good for they help us persevere when the good is difficult to attain or some evil is hard to avoid. In chapter 6 we shall look at the two classes of emotions and consider how they function in the moral life.

But ultimately passion is at the service of virtue. In chapter 7 we shall consider Aquinas's understanding of the virtues. His is not an ethic of duty or law, but an ethic of virtue. Thomas has a virtue ethic because his primary concern is not just good decisions, but good persons. Virtues are moral skills that make both actions and persons good. In Christian language, they are transforming activities that sculpt us into people capable of finding bliss in God. Virtues formed from charity transfigure us in holiness; with them we radiate the goodness of God. In this chapter we will consider what the virtues are and why we need them. We will study how they are gained but also how they can be lost. Our look at Thomas's account of the virtues will convince us that human beings are creatures who can go to extremes. Poised between epic possibilities, we are capable of extraordinary goodness, but also of terrible evil.

But can we ever be good enough? Thomas says not quite, especially when the goodness we seek is God's. In a sense, Thomas sets us up. He tells us we will never find joy unless we have union with God. But we can only enjoy such intimacy with God when we have enough likeness to the goodness of God to make such a relationship possible. Try as we might, we can never render that goodness ourselves. There is a sense of futility smuggled into Aquinas's treatise on the virtues. The virtues are perfecting, but not perfecting enough. They make us good, but not good enough. They change us, but not enough to give us union with God. We sense the possibility of virtue, but also its limitations. This is why Aquinas's account of the moral life does not end with the virtues, but with the Gifts of the Spirit. At the limit of every virtue the Gifts emerge, for it is in them that the virtues find their completion. What the Gifts of the Spirit remind us is that for Aquinas the moral life begins in gift and ends in gift. It begins with the outpouring of God's gracious love in our hearts, and ends with the outreach of God's love to complete our virtue with a goodness we could never offer, but only receive. Seeing the link between charity's virtues and the Gifts of the Spirit will give an unexpected twist to Aquinas's ethics and bring our investigation to a surprising conclusion. We shall reflect on all this in chapter 8 by looking first at the special relation every virtue has to charity, then by examining the cardinal virtues, four virtues Thomas sees as especially prominent in the moral life, and finally by thinking about the Gifts of the Spirit, those special manifestations of God's redemptive love that perfect us and guide us home.

A word about the style of this book. Studies of Aquinas's ethics have often been forbidding. The language is strange to us, the style is foreign. I have tried to make this book as accessible as possible, writing in a way that is hopefully clear and understandable but, at the same time, does justice to the spirit of Thomas's thought. References to secondary sources are few. I have avoided them not only because commentaries on Aquinas often obscure more than they illumine, but also because the best way to appreciate Aquinas's thought is to work with the texts themselves. I have focused almost exclusively on his moral treatise in the *Summa Theologiae*. Thomas wrote on morality elsewhere, but the *Summa* presents the most developed and complete account of his ethics. Where necessary I have included passages from the *Summa* to illustrate that my treatment is faithful to Aquinas's thought; however, wherever passages are cited, I have tried to explain and interpret them as clearly as possible.

Every book is a debt to those who teach us what we did not know. I am especially grateful to Sebastian MacDonald, C.P., who introduced me to the writings of Aquinas when I was a student at Catholic Theological Union in Chicago. It was MacDonald's high respect for Aquinas that prompted me to investigate a theologian I otherwise might too quickly dismiss. I am also indebted to Stanley Hauerwas, now of Duke University, who was my mentor at the University of Notre Dame. It was Hauerwas's conviction that Aquinas's ethic of virtue was the richest lore of the Catholic moral tradition that encouraged me to study him more patiently.

I must also thank the students of Catholic Theological Union in Chicago. I have taught a class in the ethics of Aquinas for several years. The classroom is a fine place to test one's ideas. It was through the persistent and perceptive questions and challenges of the students that I came to a better sense of a theology I thought I understood.

Special thanks is also due Kenneth O'Malley, C.P., of Catholic Theological Union for his painstaking assistance in preparing the text for publication.

Finally, I want to thank Lawrence Boadt, C.S.P., of Paulist Press. He convinced me a more accessible contemporary study of Thomistic ethics might not be a bad idea. It was his interest, encouragement, and enthusiasm that gave me confidence to write this book.

1. Meeting a Man with Designs on Us

No one can meet Thomas Aquinas and remain unchanged. To read him is to prepare to be transformed, to study his theology is to risk becoming someone else. Thomas does not just want to teach us, he wants to challenge us. His hope is not only that we learn, but that we become better. Thomas wants to make us holy; that is why to begin an exploration of his vision of the moral life is to begin a journey of conversion. We cannot wander the *Summa* and remain untouched. To consider its questions is to be lured, to agree with its conclusions is to be one step closer to Thomas's vision of our happiness. Thomas's moral theology has designs on us—any grand theology does—because its goal is to help us see what Thomas takes to be the utmost possibility for our lives: the surrender of ourselves in friendship to the God who is our happiness and our joy. Aquinas's moral theology implicates us in conversion because to follow his argument is not only to learn, but to enter a way of life that makes us more than we were before. To read him is to be opened to a life of grace and virtue leading to communion with God. To listen to him is to begin to understand why the goal of our life is to say yes to a God who is forever love. Yes, Aquinas's moral theology has designs on us. Its strategy is to mold us into the kinds of people who love God wholeheartedly, for as Aquinas knows, our joy is always in proportion to our love. Thomas will lead us on a journey from which, hopefully, we shall never fully recover. It is good to know him as best we can.

I. A LOOK AT THE LIFE
OF THOMAS AQUINAS

Thomas was born in the castle of Roccasecca near Aquino, a small town between Rome and Naples in the Kingdom of Sicily. He was the youngest son in a family of minor nobility. His father, Landulf, was Count of Aquino, and his mother, Theodora Theatis, was a

7

noblewoman of Norman descent from Naples.[1] The exact date of Thomas's birth is uncertain, falling somewhere between March 8, 1224, and March 7, 1225, though most scholars place his birth in 1224. Thomas had five sisters and three brothers.

After his fifth birthday (1230–1231), Thomas was taken to the Benedictine Abbey of Monte Cassino. There his parents presented him as an oblate in the Benedictine way of life, hoping he would some-day be abbot of Monte Cassino. It is important to note that Thomas, a mere child, did not profess vows as a Benedictine, but was to be edu-cated by the monks of Monte Cassino, introduced to Benedictine spiri-tuality, and gradually initiated into the Benedictine way of life. As an oblate, Thomas "was offered to God in the Benedictine way of life for elementary training in the practice of the rule and basic education."[2] He was never officially a Benedictine, but as an oblate he was dedi-cated to God under the rule of St. Benedict and was to be guided and trained by the Benedictines. To be sure, they were his first introduc-tion to religious life.

Thomas remained at Monte Cassino until 1239 when, at the urging of the abbot, he began his studies in the liberal arts and philosophy at the University of Naples, the first state university of the Western world.[3] It was here that Thomas was first introduced to Aristotle, who was to have such an impact on his own philosophy and theology. What was Thomas like at this time? James A. Weisheipl describes him as being "somewhat taller than most of his Italian contemporaries, and somewhat corpu-lent,"[4] the latter being a characteristic that would mark him through life. At the time, Bernard Gui wrote of Thomas: " 'He was a quiet boy with an unusually mature bearing; saying little, but already thinking much; rather silent and serious and seemingly, much given to prayer.' "[5] Appar-ently reticence and recollection characterized Thomas throughout his life. For instance, Josef Pieper notes that "a prayer has come down to us in which Thomas asks that it may be given him 'to be serene without frivolity and mature without self-importance.' "[6] Too, at this point Thomas already had gained a reputation for having terrible handwriting, apparently because his writing could not keep pace with his thoughts. Whatever the reason, Weisheipl observes that "only a handful of scholars in the world today can read this handwriting."[7]

Thomas Enters the Dominicans: The "Dumb Ox" Discovered

In 1243 Thomas's father died. In April of the following year, when Thomas was nineteen, he received the Dominican habit. Thomas first encountered the Dominicans in Naples. They were a mendicant order, and he could see the friars wandering the streets of Naples begging. The poverty of the Dominicans impressed him, and so did the zeal they displayed in their preaching and teaching. But Thomas's family was not so enthused. They still hoped he would become abbot of Monte Cassino and were not to be easily deterred. A month after Thomas was vested in the Dominican habit, he was abducted from the friary by his brothers and imprisoned in the family tower, where they hoped he would change his mind. According to legend, it was at this point that Thomas's brothers sent a young woman to his cell to seduce him. As Weisheipl records, "Finally one day the 'brothers' induced a ravishing girl, seductively attired, into his cell to seduce him and thereby break his will. Indignant over this attempt, Thomas picked up a burning stick from the fire and drove the girl from his room. Having then made the sign of the cross on the wall with his charred stick, he fell into a deep sleep and two angels came to comfort him, girding him with a cord of angelic purity."[8] Many biographers question whether this incident ever happened, but it illustrates two things. First, there was nothing Thomas's family could do to break his will; he was determined to be a Dominican, and realizing this, they finally relented. Second, it underscores the importance of purity or chastity in Thomas's life. For Thomas, purity represented not so much sexual abstinence, but a kind of simplicity and singleness of heart "that was a necessary condition for recognizing truth, for seeing reality."[9]

In 1245 Thomas returned to the Dominicans, first to study in Paris, and three years later in Cologne. It was during this time that Thomas came under the tutelage of Albert the Great, a fellow Dominican and one of the foremost philosophers and theologians of the time. In commenting on the role of Albert in Thomas's life, Josef Pieper says, "Had all Europe been canvassed, no more important and more up-to-date teacher for Thomas could have been found."[10] But Thomas's talents were not immediately recognized. He was quiet, shy, and somewhat aloof; in fact, his excessive reserve and his lumbering physique had earned him the moniker, the "Dumb Ox." But eventually Thomas's brilliance became known, albeit somewhat accidentally. Apparently, a fellow student thought Thomas a little dense, took pity on him, and offered to help him with his studies. "In all humility," Weisheipl writes, "Thomas accepted this help with gratitude. But no sooner had the brother started his explanation when he lost the thread of the argument. To encourage the helper, Thomas proceeded with the argument step-by-step, and 'even added a number of things that the master had not explained.' Thereupon the student asked Thomas to coach him instead, which Thomas is supposed to have done with the usual caution to 'tell no one.' "[11] The student said nothing, but Albert made a discovery of his own. Thomas had dropped a sheet of his classnotes in the corridor outside his room. A student saw the notes and decided to take them to Albert who was so impressed that he remarked, " 'We call him the Dumb Ox, but the bellowing of that ox will resound throughout the whole world.' "[12]

It was not long before the world heard. Thomas was ordained in 1250 and sent to teach in Paris. Though he felt unprepared for the task, he was assigned to lecture on the *Sentences* of Peter Lombard, the standard text in theology used at the University of Paris. It was during these years that Aquinas, not yet thirty, wrote his massive and influential commentary on the *Sentences* of Lombard. Shortly after, at the request of Raymond of Penafort, a former Dominican General then living in Spain, Thomas began working on his *Summa Contra Gentiles,* a work explaining the Christian faith that could be used by Dominican missionaries working among Jews and Moslems in Spain. It is interesting to note that most of Thomas's writings were in response to requests from fellow Dominicans to meet specific needs of the community or of the church; his writings were his apostolate, his way of serving others.

Thomas in the Classroom: Teaching Was His Soul

We cannot understand Thomas unless we appreciate how essential teaching was to his life. Teaching was not a job for Thomas, it was a manifestation of his personality, an expression of his soul. For Thomas, to teach was to be himself. "In spite of the variety of assignments that were heaped upon him, and in spite of the moving around he had to do," Pieper comments, "at bottom he remained all along and wherever he was, one thing above all: a teacher."[13] In contrast to Augustine who "said of himself that he was one of those who 'write as they grow and grow as they write,' " Pieper says Thomas "was one of those who teach as they grow and grow as they teach. . . ."[14] In fact, teaching was so much a part of his life that "in the period shortly before his death, . . . he confided to his friend Reginald that he hoped to God, if his teaching and writing were now over, that the end of his life would come quickly."[15]

What was it that made Thomas such an outstanding teacher? First, he saw teaching as embodying the ideal of the Dominican life, because in teaching both contemplation (*vita contemplativa*) and action (*vita activa*) are joined. One can only teach when he or she has first grasped the truth. Doing so requires solitude, silence, prayer and receptivity, all aspects of the contemplative life. Amidst the din and distraction of his world, Thomas was able to withdraw into the "inner cloister" of his soul. It was there in silence, study and prayer that truth came to him. "The true teacher has grasped a truth for itself, by purely receptive contemplation," Pieper observes. "The teacher, then, looks to the truth of things; that is the contemplative aspect of teaching. It is also the aspect of silence, without which the words of the teacher would be unoriginal in the primary meaning of that word, would be empty talk, gesture, chatter, if not fraud."[16]

But truth is grasped in order to share, and the true teacher is one who can give to others what he or she has received. This is the second dimension to Thomas's teaching. Yes, Thomas wanted to know what is true, but he wanted the truth in order to pass it on to others, and in this he was exemplary. Thomas's genius as a teacher was that he could so well communicate what he knew, and did this by being able to remember what it was like to learn something for the first time. As Pieper explains, "Precisely this characterizes the teacher, it seems to me: he possesses the art of approaching his subject from the point of view of the beginner; he is able to enter into the psychological situation of one encountering a subject for the first time."[17] This was Thomas's gift. His devotion to his students was so strong that he could place himself in their situation. Thomas was able to recall the wonder, fear, confusion and awe that a student feels when learning something for the first time. His gift as a teacher was that he could feel what the student was feeling; that is why he knew exactly how a subject needed to be explained. As Pieper writes, "The teacher, insofar as he succeeds in lovingly identifying himself with the beginner, partakes of something that in the ordinary course of nature is denied to mature men: he sees the reality just as the beginner can see it, with all the innocence of a first encounter, and yet at the same time with the matured powers of comprehension and penetration that the cultivated mind possesses. Thomas possessed this gift in bountiful measure. . . ."[18]

Perhaps more than anything, Thomas could evoke in his students the awe he experienced when he confronted a subject for the first time. Pieper describes Thomas as "a stable and entirely open-minded young man with a tremendous receptivity of soul and spirit,"[19] and he tried to cultivate this same quality in his students. Thomas knew that "all knowledge of any depth, not only philosophizing, begins with amazement. If that is true, then everything depends upon leading the learner to recognize the amazing qualities, the *mirandum,* the 'novelty' of the subject under discussion."[20] If he could nurture in his students this sense of awe, wonder and amazement, then they, too, could truly learn. They would begin to see that study is essentially exploration, that truth can never be captured fully, and that true learners can never rest easy with what they already know. Thomas realized that to be educated is to be led into the truth, but this implies an ongoing and open-ended investigation. True learners investigate subjects they can never exhaust and come to answers with which they can never rest easy. These are the qualities that characterized Thomas the teacher, and they are what he strove to instill in his students. As Pieper summarizes:

> And it is genuine questioning that inspires all true learning. In other words, it has dawned on the learner that what really counts is never to be taken for granted, is strange, amazing, deeper than it seems to be to common sense. That, then, is what Thomas aimed at.[21]

The Years in Rome and Paris: Thomas Begins the Summa Theologiae

Life changed again for Thomas in 1261. He was sent to open a house of studies for Dominican students in Orvieto, Italy, and upon this assignment was told by his superior that he was being sent there "for the remission of his sins," though there is no inkling that this referred to specific incidents in Thomas's life. That same year Pope Urban IV established his Papal Curia at Orvieto, and developed a warm friendship with Aquinas. Urban wanted to make Orvieto a center for scholarship, and often called upon the Dominican theologians for advice. He asked Thomas to write a commentary on each of the gospels; the result was the *Catena Aurea,* and it was received as a masterpiece.

Four years later, when Thomas was forty, he was sent to Rome to open a house of studies for his province, and again told that it was for the "remission of his sins." Whatever the reason, here began the most productive period of Thomas's life. It was here that he began his magnum opus, the *Summa Theologiae.* Its genesis may surprise us. Thomas was teaching Lombard's *Sentences* to the students, and noticed many were finding it difficult. He concluded there was need for a "beginner's book" in theology, and the masterful *Summa,* probably the most monumental theological work ever achieved, was his response. It is striking that Thomas "devoted his best energies and the longest period of his life, not to a work of 'scholarship,' but to a textbook for beginners, although it was, to be sure, the fruit of the deepest absorption with Truth."[22] As Thomas wrote in the preface, the purpose of the *Summa* "was to present those things that pertain to the Christian religion in a manner befitting the education of beginners, to present the fundamentals of theology briefly and clearly." At the very least, Thomas presented them completely. Though left unfinished when he suddenly stopped writing on December 6, 1273, the *Summa* is an awesome work consisting of 512 questions, 2,669 articles, and approximately 10,000 objections with their corresponding responses.

The first part of the *Summa* was written between 1266–1268 when Thomas was in Rome, and circulated before he returned to Paris early in 1269. Thomas traveled the distance from Italy to Paris on foot, leaving Rome in late November and arriving in Paris in January. It was in Paris that Thomas wrote the second part of the *Summa,* which is considered his most original contribution to theology. He was at the peak of his energies. As Weisheipl remarks, "During the next four years Thomas worked with incredible speed and accuracy with the help of his secretaries. We are told that he ate little and slept little, devoting his energies to writing, dictating, teaching, and praying. What Thomas was able to accomplish between 1269 and 1273 defies imitation."[23] And Pieper adds, "What he wrote during those last years in Paris—once more, only three years—seems almost beyond belief: commentaries on virtually all the works of Aristotle; a commentary on the Book of Job, on the Gospel of John, on the Epistles of Paul; the great *Quaestiones disputatae* on evil, on the virtues; the comprehensive Second Part of the *Summa theologica.*"[24] His writing was so prolific during this period that he " 'used to dictate in his cell to three secretaries, and even occasionally to four, on different subjects at the same time.' "[25] One of the more striking characteristics about Aquinas, particularly notable during these years, is that he had extraordinary powers of concentration. He could become so absorbed in a question that was perplexing him that he would grow completely oblivious to what was happening around him. Weisheipl calls this characteristic *abstractio mentis* and recounts one such incident:

> There is a famous story told of Thomas, that in 1269 he was seated next to King Louis IX at a banquet; all the while he was "rapt out of himself," thinking about the Manichees, whose arguments he was then considering. Suddenly in the midst of the meal, "he struck the table, exclaiming: 'That settles the Manichees!' Then, calling his socius by name, as though he were still at study in his cell, he cried out, 'Regi-

nald, get up and write.' " Having been brought to his senses
by the prior, Thomas apologized to the king, who ordered a
secretary to take down Thomas' thoughts.[26]

A second incident is even more amusing:

> Once when a certain cardinal legate wished to meet Thomas,
> about whom he had heard much, he asked the archbishop of
> Capua, "formerly one of Thomas's pupils," to arrange a
> friendly meeting with him. Thomas was thus called away
> from his studies to talk to the two prelates who had come to
> the priory, but he "remained in his abstraction." They made
> him sit down between them, but his mind was miles away and
> he said scarcely a word to them. After a long silence, while
> they waited for him to speak, his face suddenly beamed and
> he exclaimed, "Ah, now I have it!" Meanwhile the cardinal
> legate was becoming annoyed and indignant that this friar
> gave him and the archbishop no sign of reverence; "and in his
> heart he was beginning to despise him." But the archbishop
> said to him, "My lord, do not be surprised, he is often like
> this; with a mind so abstracted that he cannot be got to talk
> whatever the company he is in." Then he took hold of
> Thomas's cappa and tugged it sharply. Thomas came to him-
> self and, noticing the prelates on either side of him, bowed his
> head reverently to the cardinal and begged his pardon, say-
> ing, "My lord, please excuse me; I thought I was still in my
> cell." Asked why he should express such exuberance in the
> state of his abstraction, Thomas said, "A beautiful idea has
> just occurred to me for the work on which I am engaged at
> present. My pleasure in this simply burst forth in delight."
> The cardinal was taken aback, but he was very pleased all the
> same by the encounter. The archbishop enjoyed telling this
> story afterward, and often did so.[27]

A Mysterious Experience, Then Death

In late April, 1272, Thomas left Paris and headed for Naples,
where he was again instructed to open a house of studies for his Dominican province. It was then that he began work on the third section
of the *Summa* dealing with the incarnation and the sacraments. From
the spring of 1272 until early December, 1273, Thomas worked assidu-
ously, even frantically; the pace was alarming. "Thomas had been

working at a high pitch for the preceding five years, ever since his return to Paris in 1269," Weisheipl comments, "when he seemed to realize in a new way the great need for his apostolate. A kind of fever seemed to possess him, so that 'he was continuously occupied in teaching, or in writing, or in preaching, or in praying, so that he devoted the least possible time to eating or to sleeping.'. . . 'It was the common view,' according to Bartholomew of Capua, 'that he had wasted scarcely a moment of his time.' "[28] But such zeal had its price. The most productive period of Thomas's life was also the most costly. As Weisheipl notes, all this led to an event from which Thomas would never recover.

> Obviously Thomas could not keep up this pace forever. Something had to give way after five years of driving himself day in and day out. Before he was forty-nine years old, he had written more than forty substantial volumes that benefited the Church and mankind. Judging from the available evidence, we can say that Thomas's health was generally excellent throughout life; his resistance and stamina were considerable. However, something happened to Thomas on December 6, 1273, that changed his whole life; three months later he died, on March 7, 1274.[29]

What happened on that December morning? Up until then Thomas had seldom wavered from a routine he had followed for years. He arose early each morning for mass. After mass, he began teaching, followed by long periods of writing, study and prayer. But that morning something happened that so affected Thomas he was unable to resume his work. It occurred during mass when Thomas "was suddenly struck by something that profoundly affected and changed him."[30] Afterwards Thomas was unable to continue writing. He had been working on the treatise on the sacrament of penance in the third part of the *Summa*. When Reginald, his chief assistant and scribe, saw that Thomas had fallen out of a pattern he had observed so faithfully for years, he urged him to continue writing, cajoling him with the assurance that the world would profit from what he had to say, but Thomas responded, " 'Reginald, I cannot.' " When Reginald became more insistent, Thomas gave the response for which he is famous: " 'All that I have written seems to me like straw compared to what has now been revealed to me.' "[31]

These are startling words from a man who had written so expansively and so profoundly. What could have happened to make Thomas count as nothing all he had so notably achieved? Why would the man who later would become the patron of Catholic scholarship resolutely dismiss the writings for which he would be universally acclaimed? It is difficult to fathom, but it is suspected that the experience Thomas underwent that December morning was both physical and spiritual. Given that Thomas seldom spoke after that morning and never returned to his reading and writing, devoting his energies solely to prayer, it is suspected that he may have suffered a stroke. Considering the rigorous, unyielding schedule he followed, that would not be surprising. But it is also thought that what Thomas envisioned that day was the beginning of his final conversion, an encounter so gripping that in light of it the value of all else paled. Whatever he saw, it was of such beauty and goodness and power that it rendered his achievements negligible. Thomas was not the same after this. What had absorbed him for so many years no longer interested him. Whereas before he had devoted himself so unflaggingly to writing and scholarship, now he could not give that a moment's attention. What he saw that December morning completely refocused his energies and redirected his cares. " 'The only thing I want now,' " he told Reginald, " 'is that as God has put an end to my writing, He may quickly end my life also.' "[32]

Thomas's prayer was not long in being answered. In February, 1274, while en route to the Council of Lyons, Thomas " 'accidentally struck his head against a tree that had fallen across the road, and was half stunned and hardly able to stand.' "[33] It was a blow from which he never recovered. Sensing death was near, he asked to be taken to the Cistercian Abbey of Fossanova. In a guest room of the abbey, he died early on Wednesday morning, March 7, 1274. He was forty-nine years old. By no means were Thomas's theological achievements immediately hailed. Exactly three years after his death, some of Thomas's teachings were condemned as "prejudicial to the faith." This was part of a conservative backlash against Thomas's use of Aristotle. Eventually, however, Thomas was vindicated. On July 18, 1323, barely fifty years after his death, he was canonized. In 1325 his orthodoxy was declared, and in 1567 he was named a "doctor of the Church." About his canonization Pieper writes:

> In connection with this we should note that, as Grabmann
> says, Thomas seems to have been the first person canonized
> for being a theologian and teacher. The forty-two witnesses
> at the canonization trial had little to report concerning extraordinary acts of penance, sensational deeds, and mortifi-

cations. In fact, they seemed to have been somewhat put out by this aspect of the problem: they could only repeat unanimously, again and again: Thomas had been a pure person, humble, simple, peace-loving, given to contemplation, moderate, a lover of poverty.[34]

A Picture and a Recurrent Prayer: A Study of a Man in Love

It may be best to end this sketch of Thomas's life with a picture. Several years ago an exhibition from the Vatican Museum of Art was touring the country. Among the paintings was a scene from the life of Thomas Aquinas. It is night, and Thomas is at prayer. This is not surprising. His biographers tell us that in the later years of his short life, Thomas had difficulty sleeping. His nights became silent vigils of prayer before a God he loved but did not always understand. Who knows what Thomas spoke from his heart those nights? Who can guess what words he might have uttered? The picture depicts one night when Thomas did not speak, but was addressed. According to legend, Thomas was kneeling before the crucifix, and Christ said to him, "Thomas, you have written well about me. What reward would you want?" "Lord, nothing but yourself," was Thomas's response.

How might this picture speak to us? First, it reminds us that Thomas saw no separation between the moral life and the spiritual life—for him they were one. It is unfortunate that in recent centuries Catholic theology has tended to split morality and spirituality, enervating the former and isolating the latter. Once this occurs morality tends to be minimalistic and spirituality elitist. An ethics divorced from the Christian spiritual life is likely to be overly juridical and legalistic, asking not what should we do to become as much like God as we possibly can, but what must we avoid if we are not to sin. The second question is important, but it does not go far enough. We learn from it what to avoid, but not what to embrace; it teaches us what we should not choose, but says nothing of what we must deeply love.

Thomas avoided this because he never considered the spiritual life to be something other than a genuinely moral life. For him, the goal of the moral life was perfect communion with God through love. Men and women make their way back to God by acquiring the virtues which bring likeness to God, virtues born from charity's love. A good moral theology, thought Thomas, was one that held forth our best and most promising possibility. A good moral theology was magnanimous, it outlined a way of life capable of greatness, one that strove for our utmost potential in goodness and love. This is what the moral theology of Thomas Aquinas attempts to capture: How ought we to live if we are not to fall short of our most blessed possibility? The whole of Thomas's moral theology is a studied attempt to answer this question. There is for him no division between the moral life and the spiritual life; they are one, and the reason is that to be moral is to be good, and to be genuinely good is to become holy. That Aquinas saw the summit of goodness in the perfection of charity explains why for him the virtues ultimately perfect us not to be citizens of this world, but of the Kingdom.

Second, the picture suggests that for Thomas morality is essentially an affair of the heart. That Thomas would want "Lord, nothing but yourself" suggests that for him becoming moral is learning to choose the right object of devotion. All of us are creatures of devotion inasmuch as we give ourself to whatever we think is going to complete us. We are naturally and essentially lovers because we are ineluctably attracted to what we think will offer the grandest and most enduring joy. We expend ourselves on what we think will quiet our desires, on what we believe will bring peace to our souls, and for Thomas that is why it is so crucial that we learn to love God more than anything else. If we study this picture we see Thomas's gaze transfixed on the crucified Lord. It is a lover's look, a lover's longing. Thomas was absorbed in Christ because it was the sovereignty of that longing that transfigured him unto holiness. Here is a man of singular, abiding passion, and it is a passion for God, an unquenchable thirst and hunger for the One in whom our fullness lies.

To understand the moral theology of Thomas Aquinas we must understand this passion, for more than anything it gave form and shape and direction to everything he did. Thomas's moral theology is governed by a relentless, all-absorbing love for God. He does have designs on us, because he wants to make us godly lovers too; he wants us to share his passion, to live his devotion, to stand in his longing. He wants us to utter that nighttime prayer, "Lord, nothing but you." Thomas's moral theology was born, not from his head but from his heart, and to understand him we must appreciate this. What drives his crystalline schema of the moral life is a vision of the God he seeks. He writes with an interest and with a passion. He wants to offer us a way of life the pursuit of which will give us eternal intimacy with God. The desire to know "Lord, nothing but you" is the cornerstone of his moral theology, its key interpretative principle. If we remember what Thomas cared most about we will understand what he is up to in the *Summa*.

Thomas wrote the *Summa* because he loved God, and like all great lovers he believed he had something fabulous to share. Thomas wrote because he was convinced there was nothing more important than to help people see that life concerns God, that to be human is to be taken up with God; more than that it is to learn to love God whole-heartedly, absolutely and unconditionally, because such a penetrating love renders the intimacy in which we find joy. The moral theology of Thomas Aquinas is nothing more than this, the impassioned, strategic plea of a man who has found joy in knowing and loving God, and wants that joy to be our own. Yes, his is a theology with designs on us, he wants us to be great lovers too. Thomas is not indifferent to the results of his work. If we travel the *Summa* and remain unchanged, then either Thomas or we have failed. His theology is designed to trans-form us, to invite us to conversion. If we remain untouched we have not understood. What Thomas is up to in his moral theology is noth-ing less than the remaking of our hearts. We will emerge from this adventure changed.

Third, this picture of Thomas keeping vigil in prayer suggests he might not have been as absolutely certain about God and ourselves as his writings sometimes convey. Making our way through the moral theology of Aquinas can be a dizzying experience. We will be dazzled by his brilliance, we will be awed by the astonishing breadth of his mind. Thomas undoubtedly was a genius and we must respect this. Walking through the *Summa* can be like exploring a crystal palace; in fact, its structure has been compared to a Gothic cathedral.[35] It is beautiful, a place of intricacy and harmony where everything is in place, nothing is scattered, nothing amiss. Indeed, the *Summa* is an awesome synthesis of philosophy and theology that remains unrivaled in our time. Thomas moves with apparent ease from one question to the next, convincing us he knows exactly where he is going. He poses a question, he examines possible objections, and then he responds to them. At times we have the impression he knows everything about God and everything about ourselves. Sometimes we may even feel that Thomas has God under his thumb, so well explained that it is not God who is the wonder, Thomas is.

But that would be a mistake. We have to distinguish between Thomas's undeniable brilliance and the unfolding story of his life. As that climactic vision on December 6, 1273 suggests, what actually seems to be true is that the older Thomas became the less he was sure, the more he studied about God and ourselves and our world, the more he wondered what he really knew. There is a paradox to Thomas's life that is both unnerving and consoling. How is it that such a brilliant man who devoted all of his mature life to exploring our relationship with God could only conclude at the end of his investigation that what he had understood was mere straw compared to what there was to know and all there was to love? It is good for us to remember that the man on whom so much Catholic theology rests—the patron of all its scholarship—is one whose closing comment on his career testified to all he did not know and so much he had not yet understood. This does not mean that Aquinas rejected his theology, but that he saw it in perspective before the God he grappled to fathom. Thomas's learning taught him this: every light of insight is embraced by a larger mystery whose darkness draws us on.

People who awake in the middle of the night to pray are not people for whom no question remains. The searching, the restless, the stalked, and the uneasy are those who keep vigil in prayer. They pray because they must. They pray because they realize so much of their life is pierced by a mystery as appealing as it is confounding. These are the ones whose life has a touch of fear to it. This is the kind of man Thomas was. We can be sure that what happened in his life turned up in his theology. We will notice when we walk with him that there is less emphasis on what we must do and more emphasis on what God can do. We will notice less talk about human action and more attention to the agency of God. We will notice that the virtues have a peculiar strategy for Thomas, not to make us independent, but to enable us to surrender to the love that can do infinitely more for us than we ever can do for ourselves. When we get to know Thomas we will not be surprised that the moral life for him climaxes, not in certainty but in wonder, not in clarity but in worship, not in grand control but in the confidence of being loved.

It is said that in the final years of his life Thomas turned more and more to a favorite verse of the psalms for prayer. There was nothing complicated about this prayer, nothing particularly lofty, but it was the prayer of Thomas's troubled heart. Thomas prayed, "Reject us not in the time of old age," and often would say these words with tears rolling down his cheeks. Who knows what gave birth to this intercession, but it is a prayer that helps us understand the man. This is not the prayer of a man who feels he has heaven won, but of a man who hopes he never loses the God he loves. It is the prayer of a lover, but it is not the prayer of the trouble-free. Perhaps it is a good image with which to begin our adventure, this image of an aging man keeping heartfelt vigil in prayer, because it reminds us that the church has invested much in someone faith-filled but searching, hopeful but unsure, loving but always longing.

More than anything, it tells us we are about to do theology with someone very much like ourselves.

II.   A LOOK AT THOMAS'S MASTERPIECE: THE *SUMMA THEOLOGIAE*

If we are to investigate the moral theology of Aquinas as it is presented in the *Summa Theologiae,* it is important that we understand the scope, intention, and style of this masterpiece. As mentioned above, the *Summa* is composed of three parts. The first part or "Prima Pars" focuses on the existence and nature of God, the Trinity of Divine Persons, and the creation of all life from God: angels, the universe, and humankind. In the first part of the *Summa* Thomas deals with God and the coming forth or procession (*exitus*) of all creatures from the life of God. The second part or "Secunda Pars" focuses on how men and women who are created by God are to find their way back to God. How should we live if we are to return to the God for whom we are made? This is the thrust of the second part of the *Summa,* and it is broken down into two sections. In the first section of part two (Prima Secundae), Thomas deals with how we make our way back to God through our behavior and actions; it is here that he speaks of the virtues in general. The second section (*secunda secundae*) of part two is more specific. Here Thomas deals with the various virtues that draw us closer to God—the theological virtues and the cardinal virtues—and the vices that turn us away from God. Finally, in the third part of the *Summa* (Tertia Pars) Thomas deals with Christ as the one who shows us the way to eternal life, and the sacraments that are our means of salvation. Usually the first part of the *Summa* is designated by the roman numeral "I." The first section of the second part is designated "I-II," the second section of the second part as "II-II." The third part of the *Summa* is designated by the roman numeral "III." Since our reflections will focus on the second part of the *Summa,* it would be helpful to see in more detail the topics Thomas treats there. Weisheipl provides a good outline of both sections of part two of the *Summa:*[36]

Humanity's Return To God

I-II. Our movement toward God by human actions in general (Prima Secundae):

A. Ultimate goal of human life (qq. 1–5)
B. Means of attaining this goal:
    1. Human acts in themselves (qq. 6–48)
    2. Principles of human acts:
        a. Intrinsic principles: habits (qq. 49–89)
        b. Extrinsic principles: law and grace (qq. 90–114)

II-II. Our movement toward God by human acts in particular (*secunda secundae*):
  A. Theological virtues (with vices and gifts)
    1. Faith (qq. 1–16)
    2. Hope (qq. 17–22)
    3. Charity (qq. 23–46)
  B. Cardinal virtues (with vices and gifts)
    1. Prudence (qq. 47–56)
    2. Justice (qq. 57–122)
    3. Fortitude (qq. 123–140)
    4. Temperance (qq. 141–170)

As this outline suggests, each section of the *Summa* is broken down into a series of questions dealing with various aspects of whatever theme is being considered. For instance, when Thomas investigates the meaning of happiness, he first explores whether or not our actions betray a larger purpose or goal we are seeking in life. He concludes that they do and names this purpose happiness. Then he wonders what happiness might be, so he asks about "objective beatitude" or the essence of happiness. Finally he explores the conditions of happiness—what do we need in order to be truly happy?—and how happiness is gained.

But each of the questions of the *Summa* is broken down into various articles that explore relevant dimensions of the question. For instance, in question 2 of the Prima Secundae Thomas wants to know in what genuine happiness consists, and he investigates this in eight separate articles. In article 1 of question 2, Thomas wonders if happiness lies in riches, in article 2 he asks if it is found in honor, in article 3 he wonders if happiness is fame and glory. So far, then, we have seen that the *Summa* consists of three major parts. Each part contains a multitude of questions exploring various topics or concerns, and each question is broken down into a number of articles. For instance, Thomas's reflections on whether objective beatitude consists in riches occur in article 1 of the second question of the Prima Secundae. A reference to this question and article would be given as "*ST*, I-II, 2,1." Or if we wanted to see what Thomas has to say about the virtue of charity, we would turn to question 23 of the Secunda Secundae. If we were interested in his analysis of charity as the form of the virtues, we would look at article 8 of question 23. A shorthand version of writing this would be "*ST*, II-II, 23,8."

But the structure of the *Summa* is more involved than this. When Thomas explores the various dimensions of the moral life he does more than simply present his opinions. He does not begin with what he thinks, he begins with what other people have thought; he gives opposing views their due. For instance, when he wonders if happiness lies in wealth, Thomas first considers some of the reasons we might answer yes. He wants his treatment of various questions to be as fair and balanced and complete as possible. After listing other people's positions on a question, Thomas offers his own. In the case of happiness, Thomas does not conclude that happiness consists in money, but he wants us to know why. It is here that we get his substantive view on why money is not enough for happiness and what he thinks happiness must be. Finally, Thomas concludes each article by responding to the opposing views he has considered. What we notice in each of these responses is that Thomas seldom dismisses them completely; rather, he looks for whatever truth they may possess even if he cannot wholly espouse them.

How To Read the Summa

Reading the *Summa* can be daunting. The schema of questions and articles and responses can seem overly formal and dry to us, it simply is not the way we think and write today. Too, Thomas's style is extremely sparse, even austere. There is none of the passion and embellishment we find in Augustine, none of the poetry and images Bonaventure gives us. This can make the *Summa* seem brittle and dull. Its language and format can seem so far removed from us that we wonder if we can connect with it at all. At times Thomas's writing seems a disservice to his thought.

But we should be patient. It takes time to grow acquainted with any major thinker. Remember what it was like the first time we read Shakespeare or George Eliot, or how overwhelmed we were with the opening pages of Joyce's *Ulysses?* To understand a major thinker we have to let their thought and style work on us. There is a kind of asceticism involved in growing comfortable with Thomas; we must allow ourselves to be disciplined by his writing. What can be difficult in becoming familiar with Aquinas is that so little of the man himself breaks through his writing; the *Summa* is not a narrative. There are no personal asides, no revealing intimations. Unlike Augustine, Thomas cannot be recognized behind his words. This may disappoint us but it was a deliberate tactic of Aquinas. As Pieper explains, "Thomas wishes to communicate something else entirely, and that alone; he wishes to make plain, not his own inner state, but his insight into a given subject."[37]

There is a sobriety and austerity to Aquinas's writing, but that is not necessarily a defect. Thomas did not want to write about himself; he wanted to write about what he came to think was true. He did not want to explore the inner workings of his own soul; he wanted to explore reality in all its richness and diversity. He wanted us to grasp the substance of his argument as clearly and concisely as possible, this is why his style is so lean. Thomas did not want his search for the truth to be clouded by his own desires or inclinations; he did not want to stand in the way of the truth, he wanted to present the truth. Thomas wrote to help us see better, which is why his style is so simple and straightforward. He wrote to invite us to question and explore with him. He did not write to present us with answers; he wrote to invite us to become part of a dialogue, partners in an exploration. This is why Pieper says "Thomas seems to agree with Goethe in that, faced with the choice, he will always prefer the less 'inflated' expression. He avoids unusual and ostentatious phraseology."[38]

The best way to enter into the text of the *Summa* is not to see it as a barren landscape of succinctly stated questions and articles, but to realize that what we have here is an ongoing dialogue of which Thomas wants us to be a part. We cannot understand the *Summa* unless we enter into it and become a conversation partner with Aquinas. To read the *Summa* aptly we must enter a dialogue not only with Aquinas, but also with Job, Pliny, Cicero, Aristotle, Boethius, Augustine, Plato and everyone else he considers. In this respect, the *Summa* is not a finished project, it is an ongoing exploration of the whole of reality that Thomas invites us to join. We can appreciate the *Summa,* not when we read it at arm's length, but when we allow ourselves to be lured into its world and its concerns. We will even enjoy the *Summa* if we let ourselves grapple with the same questions and issues Thomas did, listening to him and others, but wondering about these things ourselves. For all its clarity and brilliance, Thomas never believed the *Summa* was the final answer on anything; in fact, its very structure suggests Thomas's conviction that our search for the truth is open-ended and forever incomplete. In this respect, we are not to read the *Summa,* we are to continue it.

The Form of the Summa

As with many of his writings, the *Summa* takes the form of a disputation (*disputatio*) or debate. This was not novel to Thomas, it was a format that characterized teaching and writing in the twelfth and thirteenth centuries. But Thomas did simplify it. "When Thomas, around the middle of the thirteenth century, took up the already well-developed instrument of the scholastic *disputatio* in order to play his own melody upon it," Pieper writes, "the first thing he had to do was to change it: to omit, to simplify, to prune. The preface to the *Summa theologica* speaks of the 'excessive accumulation of needless questions, articles, and arguments'; and Thomas, as Grabmann observes, vigorously sweeps under the table a vast number of the by then customary schoolmasterly over-subtleties."[39] Thomas reduced the traditional format of the disputation to four essential elements: 1) the formulation of the question being discussed; 2) treatment of the opinions and viewpoints of others; 3) a systematic statement of the author's own position; 4) a response to each of the opposing arguments.

Though it takes time for us to become comfortable with the format of the disputation, the concern that shaped its structure is forever timely. For Thomas and the other great thinkers of his age, learning demanded what Pieper calls a "full openheartedness to the truth of things."[40] The goal of the disputation was not to win an argument but to discover the truth. That is why the tone of the *Summa* is so even-handed and sober. Thomas writes, not to conquer his opponents or to appear more clever than they, but to converse with them in a mutual seeking of the truth. This is why Pieper says, "When a person speaks in the spirit of genuine *disputatio,* his primary wish is to clarify the substance," and adds, "Arbitrary, eccentric, and esoteric jargon is contrary to the spirit of genuine debate."[41] Perhaps one reason the style and format of the *Summa* is remote to us is that it lacks the shrill, polemical tones of so much of our contemporary discussions. One often has the impression that the goal of debate today is not to come to a better understanding of the truth, but to ridicule one's opponent. It may also explain why so many of our contemporary debates go nowhere. They are interminable not primarily because their subject matter is complex, but because unlike the medieval disputation, their goal is not a clearer understanding of the truth, but the destruction of one's opponent. The focus of the disputation was not the personality of one's opponent, but the subject both were committed to understand. This may explain why Thomas and his contemporaries were able to make progress toward the truth, while so many current discussions hardly seem concerned with the truth. Pieper offers a nice summary of the style and focus of the *disputatio:*

> In true disputation this other person is neither ignored by the speaker, nor bluffed, nor merely "worked over," spellbound, misled or, to put it crudely, "done in." Men who want not so much to clarify as to create a sensation are unfitted for debate—and they will avoid it. That point was, as a matter of fact, made as early as the twelfth century in defense of the *disputatio.* The disputation, it was held, was an excellent means of unmasking empty noise, oratory, "belletristics," and rhetoric, of keeping such devices from obstructing the search for truth and of repressing those who were not interested in the *scire* but in the *sciri,* not in knowing but in being known.[42]

Why the Truth Is Something We Do Together

Lurking behind this genre is a conviction about how one arrives at the truth. The disputation reflects the belief that truth is something no one arrives at alone, but only through ongoing conversation with others. We come to truth not singly but collaboratively, and the structure of the disputation reflects this. Thomas does not list the viewpoints of his opponents in order to quell them, but because he considers his opponents fellow seekers of the truth. Moreover, he treats their opinions respectfully, precisely because he knows there is much truth in what they say. Even though he finally articulates his own position differently, Thomas acknowledges that no one can grasp the complete truth of a subject. This is why we need to include the viewpoints of others in formulating our own. No one of us has the truth; rather, each of us comes to some insight about the truth. Thomas, for example, may not always agree with Plato, but he knows there is some truth to what Plato says. Put differently, he needs the truth of Plato's insight in order to better formulate his own. The *Summa* reflects that coming to the truth is a communal activity. We need the insights, corrections, and contributions even of our adversaries—perhaps especially of our adversaries—if we are to see more clearly what a given subject involves. Pieper summarizes well the epistemology behind the disputation:

The first point is this: Anyone who considers dialogue, disputation, debate, to be a fundamental method for arriving at truth must already have concluded and stated that arriving at truth is an affair that calls for more power than the autarchic individual possesses. He must feel that common effort, perhaps the effort of everybody, is necessary. No one is sufficient unto himself and no one is completely superfluous; each person needs the other; the teacher even needs the student, as Socrates always held. In any case, the learner, the student, contributes something to the dialogue along with the teacher.[43]

That Thomas saw the need for others in formulating his own conclusions is seen in the very careful, respectful way he articulates their positions. The disputation was a dialogue, and dialogue "does not mean only that people talk to one another, but also that they listen to one another."[44] Thomas listens carefully to what other people have to say, and he does so not to catch the weak spots in their arguments, not even to refute their arguments, but in order to glean from their position whatever is true. He knew, as Pieper puts it, that "in every serious utterance by an opponent some one of the many facets of reality is expressed."[45] We sense this in the extraordinary respect Thomas has for other people's thinking. Even if he disagrees with someone, he states their position in the clearest, most favorable, and strongest possible terms.[46] Never does he twist or distort their argument, never does he put it forward in a way that makes it easy for him to prevail. On the contrary, Thomas is so fair in formulating their positions that he makes them sound plausible and reasonable, he gives them the benefit of the doubt, so much so that we can find them quite convincing; in fact, sometimes he presents their position more clearly and convincingly than they do![47] Thomas epitomizes what Paul Valéry says must characterize anyone who debates, not to prevail, but to understand: " 'The first thing to be done by a person who wishes to refute an opinion is this: he must make it his own somewhat better than the person who best defends it.' "[48]

Why It Matters That the Summa *Stands Unfinished*

Before we embark on our investigation of the moral theology of Aquinas, one thing more must be said about the *Summa:* it stands unfinished. It is unfinished in the obvious sense that Thomas stopped all his writing and study on December 6, 1273, the day he declared,

"All that I have written seems to me nothing but straw compared with what I have seen and what has been revealed to me." At that point he had been working on the section of the *Summa* dealing with the sacrament of penance.

But the *Summa* stands unfinished in a second and perhaps more important sense. Thomas never considered it to offer a final and comprehensive answer on anything; rather, as with all his writing, he meant it to "throw open the gates to an infinitude of further seeking."[49] This may seem shocking when we consider the amazing breadth and thoroughness of the *Summa;* however, Thomas touched on so much, not because he believed he knew everything, but because he found everything so immensely fascinating. It was his enduring sense of amazement, not his certitude, that accounts for the breadth of his writings. A fundamental conviction for Thomas was that all our knowledge is fragmentary, incomplete, and in need of revision and correction.

Furthermore, it is ironic that someone who presents us with such a systematic explication of theology in the *Summa* harbored an extreme suspicion of systems.[50] With all his scholarship, Thomas began with the premise that we can never get to the bottom of things, whether that be with God, the universe, or ourselves. There is always something further to be known, something about God, our world, or ourselves that can be understood better, grasped more deeply, or more keenly appreciated. This does not mean Thomas was skeptical about our capacity to know, but it does mean he was in awe of all that can be known. The world is so rich in wonders that none of us can know it completely or finally or comprehensively; it is such a fascinating, intriguing, and alluring world that it continually invites us to further scrutiny and amazement. As Pieper says so well, "St. Thomas does not hold the thesis that neither God nor things are knowable. On the contrary, they are so utterly knowable that we can never come to the end of our endeavors to know them. It is precisely their knowability that is inexhaustible."[51] This is why learning is ongoing, positions must continually be revised, and cherished notions must be open to critique. The *Summa* is not a final word, it is an invitation. With "the gates thrown open," let us begin the adventure.

2. Why We Do Anything At All: A Look At Human Behavior

Morality begins in watching. This is why a good moral theologian has to be a good observer. He or she has to have a keen understanding of human nature. They must watch carefully the behavior of men and women, observing what they do, how they act, and the extraordinary panoply of their cares. A moralist must look before she writes because her task is not to control human nature but to understand it. Surely a good moralist wants to challenge us, but to do so he must first know well the people he hopes to inspire. Otherwise, morality does violence to the ones it hopes to enrich.

What makes Thomas Aquinas such an expert moralist is that he begins his investigation of the moral life not with a finely spun theory of how human beings *should* live, but with a careful perception of how they *do* live. Thomas begins by watching us, by studying carefully and respectfully how we go about our lives. He looks before he reasons, he observes before he concludes. He considers not only what we do, but why we might do it; this is why our cares, loves, and concerns mean so much to him. He immerses himself in our life and in our world. It is as one standing among us that Thomas begins to reflect on who we are and who we might be called to be. This is what is different and re-freshing and hope-filled about his view of the moral life. It is not a theory fashioned in abstraction; rather, it is an approach to the moral life that reflects Thomas's appreciation of who we are. He learns from us before he attempts to teach us. Put differently, Thomas lets us teach him before he utters a response. He learns from the stories of our lives something about what it means to be human, with its rich tapestry of cares, loves, and affections. Ultimately, this is the appeal of Thomistic ethics. It attracts us because it respects us, it speaks to us because it knows so well who we are. His is not an ideal construct of human life shoved oppressively upon us, but a compelling vision of our grandest possibility that is shaped from the people it is meant to serve. Any other approach will injure human nature, not nurture it. Thomas begins, not by considering who we should be, but discovering who we actually are. In walking alongside us, what does Thomas see? What do we teach him about ourselves? Thomas tells us in the very first question of the Prima Secundae (*ST*, I-II, 1, 1–6), and that shall be our focus in this chapter.

I. OF PERSONS AND PURPOSES

The first discovery Thomas makes about us might seem embarrassingly elementary, but it is upon this insight that his whole schema of the moral life pivots. Thomas learns that human beings are creatures with purposes. A small way to start, but an important first move. Thomas takes a close-in look at us and this is what initially strikes him. He observes us in a single day and notices not only that all of us are busy, but also that everything we do, even our relaxation, seems to be for a purpose. People have purposes; that is what he sees and it intrigues him. He watches us go about the tasks of our day, raising our children, caring for our homes, pouring our energies into people we love, and learns that behind everything we do there is a reason for doing it, that every action, no matter how simple, is born from a purpose the action is meant to achieve. It does not have to be momentous. We eat because we need to be nourished, but we prepare meals carefully because this is for people we love. We work endlessly at our jobs because we need money to survive, but we find meaning in our work because we cherish the ones we must support. A day in the life of each of us is a tapestry of activities, and each is held together by a purpose which gives it birth.

Thomas's concern is to get to the heart of who we are because he cannot begin until he knows this. When Thomas undertakes his study of morality, he is searching for the best way to describe us. What strikes at the essence of what it means to be human? What is it that captures most fittingly who a human being is? These are the questions guiding Thomas's investigation of ourselves. When he looks at us there is something quite specific he needs to have revealed. What we show him is that human beings are purposeful. This is what our everyday life articulates. This is what Thomas means when he says the most fitting description about us is to say that as human beings we are always acting for an end, for some purpose or goal we are set to achieve.[1] The purposes may be small (we need to buy a new car this year) or they may be grand (I want to love her wholeheartedly for the rest of my life), but somehow our lives are taken up with and identified through all the purposes we have. We know ourselves through the things we do, through how we expend ourselves in projects or for persons. Often we are hardly conscious of this because our purposes can become second nature to us; but if we consider carefully how we spend our time we will discover what Thomas discovered; that a human being is an array of purposes each of which represents an important element of her or his life. If we studied those purposes carefully we would gain a deep understanding of who we are and what we are trying to achieve. Our projects and purposes are barometers of our loves and devotions, they represent all those things with which we have identified ourselves, all those things that tell us who we are. We establish ourselves as persons through the purposes we have, whether they be projects of prayer, fidelity, or simply the resolution to be kind to all we meet.

We can appreciate the importance of Aquinas's point if we consider its opposite. What is it like to be without purpose? How do we feel when we have no sense of what we want? All of us can experience this occasionally, and sometimes it can be valuable, especially during periods of transition as we settle into new relationships or new responsibilities. However, to go through life without ever having discovered what we want or what we hope to achieve is deadly, because without a purpose with which we have identified ourself it is very difficult to know who we are. We begin to feel disconnected with life. Our existence seems ephemeral, rootless. Without purposes we have no way of touching life, no way of grasping its goodness. We float through our days with the sense that life is passing us by. To know what we want helps us avoid the feeling that our life is slipping away from us. We grow in and through our purposes, it is on account of them that we gain some sense of who we are. We establish ourselves through our wants, they give gist to our lives. We cannot be, at least in a moral sense, until there is something we intend. We need these purposes to give focus and direction to our lives, we need a plan of action. This is what Thomas means when he says to be a person is "to be self-acting and bringing oneself to an end . . ." (*ST*, I-II, 1,2). To be human is to stand in relationship with a variety of purposes each of which represents some indispensable good for our lives. If we take away these goods we diminish ourselves, and if we are bereft of them completely we disappear. We grow through our wants, and we grow fulsomely when our wants are good. In his excellent book, *Making Christian*

Sense, Paul L. Holmer helps us appreciate how important it is to know what we want and how dangerous it is when we don't.

> But a tragedy is in the making when a person does not learn what every person finally must learn: that is, some powerful and persistent wants. For unlike the animals whose wants are given with their very birth and nature, persons have to spend time learning what their proper wants are. And if one does not want what is essential and needful—for example, to be morally sound, to be intelligent and informed rather than stupid, or even to be healthy rather than sick—then a good part of being a person is missing. . . .
>
> Certainly a person is in dire straits if he or she has to say at the age of fifty or sixty, "I have never known what I wanted." For that state, too, describes a life without any gist, without any significance. Not to know what you want is to be bereft of direction.[2]

Intentions and What They Do to Us

Another way to appreciate Aquinas's point is to consider what it is to be an intentional being. To have an intention is to be turned toward something we seek. If we intend something we direct our intelligence and energy to securing it, and we want it because we consider it important for our lives. Everything we do is shaped by what we intend. All our actions are formed by whatever intention brings them into being; in fact, we can think of every act as having some intention to accomplish. This is what Thomas means when he says all our "deeds originate from having an aim. And so this is why they are performed" (*ST,* I-II, 1,1). The aim of every action is the intention the act is set to achieve. Everything we do originates from an intention, which is nothing more than saying actions are not pointless but purposeful, they have targets, they have goals; every act is set into play with a mission to accomplish.

Thomas offers an anatomy of human behavior. The first thing he notices about us is that we are active, we are taken up with purposes, with things we want to achieve. The second thing he notices is that behind every act is an intention, which is where an action begins. The intention alerts us to what we hope our act will accomplish. But because this is so we can say that every act begins from the end it seeks. We act because we want to gain some good. Before we act we focus on that good, we consider what it is and then we consider what we must do to attain it. This is why we can say every act takes its cue from the end it is set to accomplish. An act grows up around its intention, for it is the intention that helps us understand why we do one thing instead of another, or why our behavior might be slightly different from others. It is different because there are different intentions at work in our lives. This is what Thomas means when he writes, "Clearly, all activities a power elicits come from it as shaped by its formal interest. . . . Consequently, all human acts must be for the sake of an end" (*ST,* I-II, 1,1). The language is not our own, but the idea is one with which we can agree. All Thomas means is that everything we do bears the mark of the purpose it seeks. All action is spawned from a desire for something, which is why we can say any act really begins in the end it wants to achieve.

Why does this matter? Perhaps because it is through what we intend that we become one kind of person instead of another. Our intentions not only shape our actions, they also shape ourselves. Our purposes characterize us. Each of us carries the mark of what we most consistently will. It is not only our acts that are at stake in our intentions; we are as well. To intend to act a certain way is likewise to intend to be a certain way, the two are inseparable. Put differently, our intentions determine our actions, but they also determine ourselves; this is why so much of what becomes of us is inscribed in our choices. It is also why, for Aquinas, the most important first move in morality is attaching ourselves to a purpose worthy of ourselves, a purpose the seeking of which helps us realize our most magnanimous possibilities. What we choose as our purposes makes all the difference because invariably we become what we love. Our primary intention in life expresses what we most love. We cannot escape the influence of our sovereign love because it is what we intend in all we do. The meaning of intentional behavior is that we tend to what we most consistently love, and because we tend to it eventually we become like it, not in any superficial sense, but in the radical sense that ultimately our self is nothing more than our most perduring intentions. This is what Thomas means when he says the core intention of our life "produces a determinate effect" (*ST,* I-II, 1,2). That is right, and the "determinate effect" is ourself. What is involved in every enduring intention is the radical shaping of the self as one kind of person instead of another; we bring ourselves into being according to what we intend.

What becomes of us is determined by our power to be intentional. Why so? Because the impact of intentional behavior is a further defining of the self. Thomas recognizes a very close connection between what we do and who we become. Our intentions form our behavior, but our behavior forms our self. We can put it this way: the intention of an act gives a special quality to the act, it identifies it. But when we act, the identifying quality of the action also becomes an identifying quality of the self; the intention which forms the act also forms the person who acts, the two are internally connected. Though this might sound arcane, it explains why we eventually become what we do. Take kindness. If we perform an act of kindness once, its effect on our person is negligible. But what happens if kind behavior becomes for us a characteristic way of acting? Then it is not only our acts that are kind, we, too, are people of kindness. By habitually having the intention of being kind, and expressing that intention in our activity, we gradually shape ourselves into people who are kind. Why? Because the quality of an act of kindness becomes a quality of our selves. Eventually we act kindly because we are kind persons, kindness is one of our virtues; it is a manifestation of who we genuinely are. For Aquinas, actions and persons ultimately coalesce. We are what we do and, as we shall see, Aquinas's theory of the virtues depends on this. The intention which forms the act does not remain in the act, it passes over into the agent who acts. This is why if we do something often enough we gradually take on the quality of the action. This is why our behavior haunts us: the purpose which shapes the act also shapes the person. There is hope in this if our actions are good. It helps us understand why acting generously makes us generous people, why isolated acts of compassion truly change our soul, why people who behave lovingly truly are lovely. In each instance, the quality of the act increasingly becomes a quality of the self, and so we really are virtual expressions of what we do.

John Finnis deals with this in his book, *Fundamentals of Ethics.* Finnis argues that there are two dimensions to every act. There is the "transitive effect" and the "intransitive effect." The transitive effect is what our action achieves outwardly, it is what gets done in the world by what we do.[3] The intransitive effect is what our actions do to us. The first focuses on what behavior achieves externally, but the second considers what behavior does within us, how it changes us, how it forms our character. The intransitive effect considers how our actions constitute us as persons. As Finnis explains, "The intransitive effect is this: by a free choice I willy-nilly constitute myself a certain sort of person."[4] The intransitive effect of behavior reminds us that choices last. They don't die the moment they are enacted; they endure, and they endure not only as a state of affairs in the world, but also, and sometimes more lastingly, in the self. Our actions bring about something outside us, but they also bring about something inside us; they endure by becoming part of who we are. This means the future of every action is some aspect of our character. "One's character takes the shape of the choice one has made,"[5] Finnis writes.

Why We Become What We Most Love

All this may sound like a kind of mental gymnastics, but actually it is the key to our moral deliverance. For Aquinas, the great beauty and promise of the moral life is also perhaps its greatest fear: we do become what we most love. There is no way to escape this. We cannot avoid the influence of our sovereign desire because it abides as the primary intention in all of our behavior. It expresses itself in all we do, it is the power behind our activity. What we love most gets spoken through our actions, and through those actions returns to us in a further defining of ourselves. There is grand hope in this because it means we actually can and do become the kind of people we wish to become; action is efficacious, most notably in the character it produces within us.

For instance: What if we wish to be people of love? Thomas shows us that we shall. If charity, this passionate love for God and others, is the heartfelt intention of our lives, then it is effectively present in all we do, even if we do not consciously advert to it. This desire to love God and neighbor wholeheartedly endures as the formative desire empowering our behavior, which means that even the most ordinary activity transfigures us in the love we wish to be. This is what Thomas means when he says charity becomes the "operating principle" of every action. We may not think of some tedious everyday chore as a manifestation of charity, but if it is born from the love by which we seek to guide our lives, then charity shines through what we do and transforms who we are. If, as Aquinas suggests, all our behavior is shaped by whatever intention is primary to our lives, then everything we do, however varied, will display a certain consistency, then all our actions, however unique, will together form the single action of our lives. This is what Thomas means when he writes, "Moreover, to aim at an end is to direct activity towards it" (*ST*, I-II, 1,2).

This is why the intention threading all of our behavior gives a unity and coherence to our lives. This is why we can look at all the piecemeal actions of our day and see them not as scattered, chaotic behavior, but part of a single overriding action to which each contributes. Such behavior, however trivial, is never purposeless because it contributes to the overall tapestry we are weaving for our lives. In short, what saves everyday behavior from futility is our awareness that it is more than everyday, our sense that through the power of our most abiding intention we enable it to contribute to the purpose we have given to our existence. Whatever stands as our fundamental purpose or aim in life will be the ultimate causal force of our actions. Everything we do feels the influence of this primary intention, every act in some way is a vessel of our basic love. This is why all our behavior, no matter how prosaic, forms the single ongoing action of our lives done a certain way. It is through the power of intention that we are able to make every act part of the overall plan we want for life.

But because the character of every act returns to shape the character of the agent, people whose deeds are born in the crucible of charity eventually become great lovers themselves. We are changed according to what we do; that is why when we intend to act a certain way we ineluctably intend to be a certain way. Put simply, why do we strive to shape all our behavior in genuine love? Because we want to be true lovers ourselves, because we want love, not to be an ornament of the self, but the most fitting articulation of our being. We want to be love in heart and soul. That is why the genuine love of charity remains the pivotal intention of everything we do. What is more, we intend charity because we sense that in seeking it we really do become it. We act in love because we believe actions are efficacious, we are convinced that through habitually behaving a certain way we really do remake ourself according to what we hope most to be. We act because intuitively we sense what Thomas proclaims: we are changed according to what we most consistently intend, we are formed in its goodness, shaped in its love. The great reassurance of Thomistic ethics is that we shall not fall short of what we seek because to seek it is to be remade according to it. We shall possess what we love in the most radical way possible—we shall become it.

II.   SEARCHING FOR THE GOOD IN WHICH WE DESIRE NO MORE

But Thomas still has not told us enough. He has told us that we are purposeful, active creatures. He has learned from us that everything we do we do intentionally. And as he has observed us he has learned that we act a certain way because we want to be a certain way. But he still has not seen clearly through to who we are. When Thomas begins his observation, he takes a close-in look at life. He perceives us in the finest detail of our behavior. He walks with us through daily life trying to understand why we do what we do. But he needs to step back to gain a more panoramic view of the world. He needs to probe more searingly into what it is that drives human life, what it is that causes us to strive for anything at all, and why it is that apathy is the most unnatural state into which we can fall. Thomas needs to take that long contemplative look at human behavior in order to see to our depths and learn there what might be the most basic thing we share in common. What is it that makes the world one?

Thomas takes a second look at us and this time from a further distance away. He sees us not singly but collectively. He spies not particular actions but the storied history of human behavior everywhere. He is looking for the most elementary motive for all human behavior; he is struggling to grasp the most adequate explanation for our lives as purposeful. Taking away what would bring all human activity to a halt? Posing that question allows Thomas deeper insight into the mystery of human activity. What does there have to be in order for us to do anything at all? In what do we have to believe for our life's activity not to be absurd?

Thomas says there has to be an ultimate end. There has to be some good in which we see ourselves completed, something so lovely it will bring peace to our desires. As he puts it, ". . . in all things whatsoever there is an appetite for completion, the final end to which each moves marks its own perfect and fulfilling good" (*ST,* I-II, 1,5). For Thomas, there is in each of us a hunger for wholeness, an undying desire for some condition in which we want no more, and for each of us the ultimate end is whatever we think will achieve this. Human beings are seekers of completion, people who relentlessly, often tragically, pursue whatever they think will ultimately content them. We strive for these things, we devote so much of our energy and attention to possessing them. If we reflect back on our lives we discover how we chased after whatever we thought would be eminently good for us. Our lives are strategic endeavors to be united to what we think will bring us to completion, and whatever that is will be our ultimate end. The ultimate end is what we take to be our most perfect good, our most satisfying possibility. It is the one thing we seek for its own sake, not for the sake of anything else. The ultimate end represents what each of us takes to be our most perfecting possibility. What do you believe is your greatest good? To what are you most consistently turned because you believe it is best for you? Answering these questions gives us our ultimate end. It is our most endearing object of devotion, and we expend ourself on it because we believe that in possessing it we shall find joy. This is why Thomas says we are all one inasmuch as there is something which functions for each of us as an ultimate end, but we are not all one about what this good might be; that is why not everyone agrees on that in which complete fulfillment is found. But practically all of us devote our energies to pursuing what we think is best for us, and our ultimate end is whatever that is.

Morality Begins in a Sense of Incompleteness

Why does Thomas believe this? Because for him the moral life begins in the perception that there is something crucial we lack. Morality begins in the awareness of our incompleteness, the shattering recognition that we are far from whole. There is something missing, something to complete us we have yet to possess. The moral life stirs in the first awareness of our indigence. We are not all we can be, we are radically and often painfully incomplete. We sense this in moments of loneliness. We feel it powerfully when a shot of sadness chases our deepest joy. We experience it when we feel restless and discontent but are not sure why. What we are experiencing, Thomas would say, is the soul-felt awareness that there is something integral to ourselves that we need but do not have. The human spirit is driven by a hunger for wholeness, it is fired by the unquenchable desire for a healing of our brokenness, a restoration of the fragmented self. No matter what we have, this is the "more" we always desire, it is the longing that haunts every activity. We live in search for that final satisfaction in which we shall want no more.

This is why we come to the heart of Aquinas's moral theology when we see that, for him, morality begins in a stirring of desire. It is desire for the good we believe holds forth our completion. Morality is about desire—for Thomas, it is about love, that unquenchable passion for something to fill our hearts and bring peace to our souls. We are searchers. We are scavengers for some goodness to content us, some promise that will make us desire no more. As Thomas sees it, desire is what moves us to action. Take away desire, he says, "and no one would begin to do anything. The plan starts with the final aim; the performance with the first step towards it" (*ST,* I-II, 1,4).

Those are cryptic but crucial words. The plan of our lives begins with its final aim. And for Thomas that final aim is what stands for us as our ultimate end. In what do we see ourselves completed? How we answer that tells us for what we are aiming in everything we do. All our activity is covertly directed to whatever good we think will complete us. When we begin to act we initiate our first step to our final goal. This is why Thomas says, "an object on which his desire finally rests dominates a man's affections, and sways his whole life" (*ST*, I-II, 1,5). Inevitably, our life is bent on wholeness; that is why we are turned in everything to what represents our culminating good, and why our desire for some ultimate good will get expressed in all we do. What Thomas suggests is that we have to believe that such a good not only truly exists, but also can really be attained. If we do not believe there is some good that will heal us, restore us, and make us whole, some good that will be a balm for our broken souls, eventually, Thomas says, we will despair of acting at all because we will be convinced the very thing for which all our actions ultimately hunger is fantasy. Or else if we conclude that some such sovereign good exists but remains hopelessly out-of-reach, we shall die in the conviction that purposeful behavior is finally absurd. We act because we desire, but also because we believe that ultimately those desires can be satisfied. As Thomas writes so knowingly, "Were there no ultimate end, nothing would be desired, no activity would be finished, no desire would come to rest" (*ST*, I-II, 1,4).

The Moral Life Is a Journey to Find Peace for Our Souls

And so, for Thomas, the moral life is not only a journey to become good, it is also a journey to find peace. The moral life ends for Thomas when peace finally comes to our desires, when we hunger and thirst no more, when all our searching has come to an end because we finally possess the good in which we are completed. Thomas writes so probingly: "The ultimate end ought so to fulfill a man's whole desire that nothing is left beside for him to desire (*ST*, I-II, 1,5). The project of the moral life, for Thomas, is to bring us to that final resting place where we no longer have to seek because we have found, to bring us to union with a good so enriched, that in possessing it and being possessed by it, we desire no more. The moral life is the never-ending saga of searching for the good that will quiet the restlessness of our hearts. Desire gives birth to action, and we act most enduringly for what we think shall bring us fully to life. What we search for is something so grandly good that it quiets our desires, for it is in possessing it that we shall find peace and joy. Of course, Thomas is going to say such peace and joy is ours only when we love what is genuinely and perfectly good. Nothing less will satisfy us. No matter how good, nothing less will calm the restlessness of our hearts. We seek something so lovely that in possessing it we want no more. This is why it will be so important for Thomas that we learn to love the right things in the right way, and that we love most that which is exquisitely good. Nothing short of perfect loveliness will be enough for us.

But it also explains why, short of the perfect possession of this good, a certain restlessness will mark our lives. It helps us understand why what peace we have shall always be partial, and why sometimes at the moments of greatest intimacy we can feel shudderingly alone. As richly human and blessed as these moments are, they still fall short of the perfect love in union with which we shall hunger and thirst no more. There is an undercurrent of dissatisfaction in the best and happiest of lives, not because such happiness is counterfeit, but because even in its genuineness it is incomplete. This is part of every human life and though frustrating it is not necessarily bad. It is our restlessness that often spurs us on, our dissatisfaction that compels us to search for something better. It is because every joy lures to greater joyfulness and every union harkens to a communion in which all divisions cease that we continue to desire, act, and hope. What Thomas has shown us in his beginning observations of the moral life is that morality moves on desire, it depends on dissatisfaction, it needs restlessness. This is not the restlessness of the scattered or distracted, but the restlessness of the not yet, the restlessness of the something more. It is this restlessness which moves us to act, to search, to seek, to scrutinize. And it is often through this restlessness that we come to discover the one object truly worthy of our affections, the goodness so complete that it deserves the gift of our lives.

Why Anything Good Is Good

And yet saying we yearn for some fulsome good in no way discounts the splendor of the goods we enjoy now. By speaking of some ultimate good in which joy and peace are found, some good so exquisite that in possessing it we desire no more, Thomas does not detract from the genuine goodness of all the wonders of our world; in fact, he helps us understand why they truly are good. How so? Thomas answers succinctly that everything we love and value and cherish, we do so on account of that singular good we seek most of all. What does he mean by this? First, Thomas suggests we value everything insofar as it calls our attention to or directs us more closely toward our supreme good. Something has value for us because through it we are reminded of the good we desire over all. Everything precious and beautiful and dear to us shines in intimation of what we love most. In their goodness they are hints of perfect goodness, promises of perfect peace. Secondly, Thomas sees a connection between the ultimate good and all these intermediate goods, in the sense that it is precisely the pristine goodness of our ultimate end that reveals the undeniable goodness of everything else; it is in light of our ultimate good that we rightly discern the loveliness of everything. This is why it is so important to learn to cherish what is truly good.

This is Thomas's argument. Everything that is truly good receives its goodness from what is perfectly good; its goodness is "of" the ultimate end. That is why it is genuinely lovely and why it truly is worthy of our affections. Its goodness is not counterfeit, it is real, so even if its goodness is incomplete we are not deceived when we love it. Goodness is real. And that is extremely important, immensely reassuring. All those things that beckon to us with their goodness are not fraudulent, they are genuinely good, undeniably lovely. This tells us we can have confidence in our intimation of value, that when we respond to something as good it is good. If everything that is good takes its goodness from the fulness of goodness, then we can be sure it truly is good and really is worthy of our love. The world's goodness is not counterfeit, nor its value an illusion. What we come to love as good really is good because it is both derived from and points to the consummate goodness in which we shall desire no more. That is why the peace, happiness, joy and contentment we experience here, however partial and fleeting, is nonetheless real. That it passes does not diminish its value; rather, it increases our hope. This is what Thomas means when he concludes: "And so every initial perfection anticipates the consummate perfection which comes with the final end" (*ST,* I-II, 1,6). In everything genuinely good we glimpse what is perfectly good, in everything truly joyful we get a hint of the blessedness to come.

Thomas makes two important points. First he says we come to hope for our ultimate good by experiencing it, however incompletely, through all that is good now. We savor the perfect goodness that is to come, not by passing over life or the things of this world, but through them. Sometimes we think we only can appreciate the perfectly lovable by denying or avoiding the goods that are ours now, but Thomas says that isn't so. For him, the perfect joy for which we hope is mediated through whatever joys we know now, that is why the joy, peace, and love we experience in this world are so precious. We know the perfectly lovable through all the various manifestations of loveliness in the everyday. That is how we know and experience goodness, concretely, incarnationally. We touch the perfect good for which we hope through all intermediate goods. They bring heaven home to us, they are the Kingdom under wraps.

Secondly, through the tight connection Thomas forges between the ultimate good and all intermediate goods, we learn something wonderful about human experience and its meaning. We live in a world of wonders, a world shot through with blessing and grace, because the consummate good of our lives can be and is experienced now. Everything good glistens with the promise of the good yet to come. Everything good beckons to us with hints of perfect blessedness; that is why it is good, that is why we see it as so lovely. There are intimations of blessedness in all good things; everything lovely is a foretaste of the feast to come. That is why we can believe in the goodness and love we know now, that is why we know it is real. It is our initial participation in the "consummate perfection which comes with the final end" (*ST*, I-II, 1,6). We are not deceived by genuine love, not deceived by joy and happiness. They may be passing but they are real. We can put confidence in all the things we value now because together they are reminders of a future we can be sure will be ours. The deepest value of human experience for Thomas is that it carries along inside it promises of the Kingdom to come. We desire the ultimate goodness because through the wonders of the world we have already, however incompletely, known it, and because we have known it we are confident we do not desire in vain.

Who are we? What are we about? These are the questions Thomas has tried to answer as he begins his journey to the heart of the moral life. Thomas has learned much from us. By walking with us he has moved closer to the essence of what it means for us to be. We have shown him that to be human is to be purposeful. In looking carefully, Thomas has learned that behind every action stands a purpose for which the action is done. Those purposes are important because they not only identify our actions, they also identify our selves. Eventually we become what we most seek, eventually we are transformed through our most enduring intentions. But through observing so closely Thomas has learned something more. He has discovered that the human heart is fired by the desire for wholeness and completion. There is a hunger in us for something so good that in possessing it we shall desire no more. He has watched us and discovered that whatever stands for our ultimate end holds sway over our whole lives and dominates our hearts. This is why he concludes that our moral odyssey begins in desire for this good and ends only when that desire has been brought to rest.

It is a different starting point for a treatise on the moral life, but the difference is refreshing. Thomas began by reflecting on how we live. What he has learned most is that we are motivated in all our behavior by a powerful desire for wholeness. He calls it our ultimate end. Desire for the ultimate end is something we all share, even though we may not agree on what it is. Thomas must grapple with this, and that is why the next thing he wants to discuss with us is happiness.

3. Happiness: The One Thing Everybody Wants

Anybody who promises to make us happy has our attention. We may be skeptical, but we will listen. Everyone wants to be happy, and if we doubt this we only have to recall how much of our energy is devoted to seeking what we think will bring us joy. This is why when Thomas talks about happiness we're hooked. We cannot help but want to be happy, so when Thomas tells us that "happiness is our true good," that it "is our proper and complete good," and that the most perfect happiness "essentially remains and is forever," we not only nod our heads in agreement, we want to hear more. Not to want to be happy is inhuman. All of us may slip into destructive patterns of behavior, but that is not because we spurn happiness; we simply have not yet understood where genuine happiness is found.

And that is what Thomas wants to tell us. He has watched us in our pursuit of happiness. He has seen all we chase after, thinking it will make us whole: money, pleasure, fame, honor. He has watched what our devotions do to us, how they change us, how sometimes they lift us but so often they drag us down. He has seen how we expend ourselves on whatever we think will bring us joy and he admires that, but he also wants us to be careful, for he knows we sometimes offer ourselves precipitately, giving ourselves to something not worthy of our preciousness.

That is why Thomas wants to talk to us about where true happiness lies. He wants to summon us to our most wholesome possibility for he knows that only in possessing that shall we find enduring joy. He knows when he talks about happiness he has our attention because he can count on happiness as the one thing every human being desires. We may not agree on anything else, but we do agree we want to be happy. We are seekers of happiness, but where should we search? We hunger for indefectible joy, but where is such bliss to be found? These are questions that stir the heart. Thomas asked them too, and he wants to tell us what he discovered. What is genuine happiness and where is it found? These are the things Thomas considers in each of the articles of question 2 of the Prima Secundae (*ST,* I-II, 2, 1–8) as he continues his inquiry into the moral life. They will be our focus in this third chapter.

I. WRONG TURNS ON HAPPINESS

Once more Thomas begins by watching us. He starts by making himself a student of human life. He sees quickly enough that we are seekers of happiness, but a longer meditation before the tapestry of life shows him we do not all agree what happiness is. We seek it in different places and in different ways. We are one in our desire to be happy, but amazingly scattered in how we think the search for happiness will be resolved. In many respects, Thomas learns that the moral life for all of us is best understood as this ongoing search for whatever we think will bring us joy; maybe it is nothing more than a fabled odyssey to what we think will bring us peace. Thomas learns this: much of our lifetime is an investigation into candidates for happiness. If we look back over our lives, especially before we settled into commitments and promises, we see that much of our time was an ongoing experiment with all the things we thought would bring us joy. Thomas wants to examine these possibilities carefully and he wants to take them seriously. Even though he will conclude that there is one thing alone that brings final and everlasting joy, in no way does he want to disparage all the other devotions we form. He will acknowledge their goodness and he will grant that each in some way is essential to well-being; however, he will also always be calling our attention to something more, to something all-surpassing, because he is convinced it is only in union with this that we shall find the happiness we so relentlessly seek.

It takes time to discover what happiness is. We know this because we have learned by our mistakes. We have taken wrong turns on happiness, we have pursued dead ends. Sometimes we have been irreparably wounded because we have invested ourselves so thoroughly in something we thought would be our good, only to discover we were deceived; in fact, it may be true that often we are mistaken about happiness much more than we are correct. It is natural for us to want to be happy, but none of us naturally knows where happiness is to be found. Thomas knows this. He sees we are frequently mixed-up about happiness, so often attaching ourselves to what will harm us more than bless us, sometimes expending ourselves so destructively we wonder if happiness will ever be ours. Other times we form attachments which take us somewhere, but don't take us far enough, so we feel disappointed and perhaps slightly betrayed. There is pressure on us to expend ourselves on goods that are not worthy of us, much pressure on us to give ourselves away to the wrong things, not in the sense that they are bad, but are not good enough to bring us the joy and peace we seek. From his observations on life, Thomas learns what all of us experientially know. We are naturally heroic, inasmuch as all of us give ourselves wholeheartedly to something, sacrificing our time, energy, and our self to whatever we think will bless us most. But do we sometimes pour ourselves out in vain? Are our oblations sometimes deadly?

Thomas wants to speak to us about happiness because he cares for us and wants to help us avoid these destructive choices. He knows there is a natural generosity to the human spirit, but he also knows if we give ourselves to something less than ourselves, we drag ourselves down, we diminish ourselves, and sometimes we nearly destroy ourselves and that should never happen. Happiness lies in something magnanimous, something not only capable of greatness, but something which can bring us, as Thomas puts it, to the "full and most perfect development of ourself" (*ST*, I-II, 2,4). Happiness is being related to whatever is best for us; it is lovelife with whatever good enables our most noble possibility; put differently, happiness is lifelong friendship with our most promising good. In relation to what is such fulness possible? This is the question guiding Thomas's investigation of happiness.

We can see a concern at work. Thomas fears bad attachments because he knows what they can do to us. Bad attachments come from mistaken notions of happiness, but such mistakes are not benign; they cripple us, they make us morally feeble, and if pursued they begin an interior deterioration we should desperately fear. It is natural enough to make mistakes about happiness, but we should learn from them, not embrace them. If we settle into bad attachments we disfigure ourselves, turning further away from genuine goodness and life. Bad attachments begin a decreation, for instead of inching us toward fullness of life, they pull us back into the abyss of chaos and confusion, making us the tragic antithesis of what God's love wants us to be. As we search for happiness we are bound to encounter dead ends. Our history may be a chronicle of confusion on where joy is found. Thomas knows this, and it is why he so aptly quotes Boethius: " 'Anyone who chooses to reflect on past excesses will appreciate how pleasures have sad endings' " (*ST,* I-II, 2,6). Another way of translating Boethius here is, "Whoever wishes to reminisce about misplaced desires understands that such desires leave us sad." We feel the insight. Through Boethius, Thomas calls to mind a typical and powerful human experience. So often we learn the inadequacy of our devotions through the diminishment of their returns. They do not deliver the contentment we had hoped. We place our trust in them and come up short. We leave them feeling wasted, but at least having learned that a fuller, richer happiness is not to be found there, and so our odyssey continues.

As we travel with Thomas in this search for real joy we will notice that he thinks differently, even quaintly, about happiness. Unlike so many of us, Thomas does not think happiness is the freedom to pursue and satisfy our desires, irrespective of what those desires are; that is a therapeutic notion of happiness, not a moral one. Thomas agrees happiness entails the satisfaction of desires, but he also argues that part of becoming happy involves the purification of our desires. Often we are not happy, Thomas suggests, because we desire the wrong things, or else we desire some right things in the wrong way, giving them undue devotion. For Thomas, happiness depends on cultivating the right preferences and nurturing the proper desires. We have to learn where true happiness is to be found. We have to be educated in happiness, tutored in the love from which it is derived. And in order to be happy we probably have to change ourselves.

Thomas speaks of happiness as objective, not subjective, at least in the sense that for him happiness is not an open-ended, formless concept we are free to define in whichever way we want; rather, happiness has a precise meaning; it is the nurturing in us of the best and most promising desires, the richest and noblest love. Thomas says to be genuinely happy is to possess the greatest possible good in the deepest possible way; happiness is intimacy with loveliness, but that suggests if we have not found happiness it may be because we have yet to undergo the conversion which makes it possible. In order to be truly happy we must become the kind of person who loves the good where happiness is to be found. We must learn to desire this good and seek it more than we seek anything else. Part of the disquiet of our lives may be that we are not yet the kind of people who are able to love that in which happiness lies. Put differently, Thomas has a normative understanding of happiness, not an individualistic one, and this means that in order to be happy we must be conformed to the good that offers it, we must be remade, redirected, internally transformed until we practice the love that brings true joy. Happiness hinges on becoming good.

Candidates for Happiness and Why They Fall Short

When Thomas begins his inquiry into happiness, he does not immediately tell us what happiness is; instead, he examines first what so many of us take happiness to be. He lets us begin the conversation. He lets us speak to him about where we have tried to find contentment in our lives, and he takes what we have to say seriously. Thomas watches us. He gains some initial understanding of where happiness might be by observing how we live. He studies our behavior. He apprises our objects of devotion. He considers our attachments. As before, his position is not formed in abstraction, but in response to how we actually live. It is in observing our pursuit of happiness that Thomas draws up an initial list of candidates for happiness. We can guess that Thomas will not settle with these, but he does respect them. As we shall see, he considers money, honor, fame and glory, power and pleasure each as candidates for happiness, and though he will not conclude that lasting well-being is found exclusively in any of these, he will say that a good and prosperous life must include them in some way. Thomas does not dismiss them. He considers them good, and even considers them necessary; when it comes to happiness, he takes each as far as it can go. If we think utter happiness might be rendered in wealth, Thomas will listen carefully to what we have to say because he appreciates the attractive power of wealth. If we suggest that deep happiness comes with honor and fame, Thomas will agree as far as he is able because he knows a good reputation is important in life. To a certain degree, each of these things he examines is plausible as a candidate for happiness because each is unquestionably good.

Thomas respects the hold money, reputation, power, prestige and pleasure can have on us because he respects their goodness. If he concludes that perfect happiness is not to be found in any one of them, he never concludes they have no value, nor that they do not hold an important position in any good life. If we have flirted with each of these as candidates for wholeness, Thomas does not blame us, he understands the hold such goods can have on us. He agrees there is something about each of them that goes a long way toward making our lives pleasant and good. They do provide happiness of a sort, and we would count any life lacking that would not include them at all. Thomas acknowledges how strongly all these goods can lure us, precisely because they are good. That is not the question. The question is whether any of them can carry the burden of lasting happiness, whether in any is the goodness requisite to bring peace to our hearts. This is what Thomas considers when he begins his investigation.

Since Thomas is a realist, it is not surprising that when considering candidates for happiness he begins with money. It might seem crass, but it is true that a lot of people, even if they would never admit it, live as if money is our ultimate joy. We might not want to think that about ourselves, but Thomas looks at how we structure our lives and where we expend our energy. If experience has any connection to the truth, we have to give money its due, and Thomas does. On the face of it, he says, there are many good reasons to think perfect happiness consists in being wealthy. Common sense suggests it. If we look about and see how many people live, it would not be amiss to say money is what makes people happy. Is it right to say happiness comes in wealth? Practically speaking, Thomas says yes, and the reason is so many people live as if this is true. He argues that whatever we think will make us happiest is what we allow to win our hearts and master our affections, and for many this is money. As Thomas writes, "For since happiness is man's final end it must be looked for where his affections are held above all. And such is wealth, as Ecclesiastes remarks, 'All things obey money' " (*ST,* I-II, 2,1).

Can so many be wrong? Thomas wonders about this. If we look around us, he says, there seem to be many people who believe that if they are rich they will not be disappointed. If we consider the evidence, he suggests, a majority do think that money is the one thing that won't let them down; when it comes to happiness, that is where they place their wager. If money wins the hearts of so many, must it not be true that in riches is found our ultimate joy? Are we wrong to believe that wealth is what life is about and possessions should receive our supreme devotion? There is an initial plausibility to this claim. Besides, the evidence is that money brings happiness. Look at wealthy people. Most seem fairly happy, don't they? Money has enabled them to set up a comfortable life, a life of minimum inconvenience. Not only are they able to do what they want whenever they want, they are also able to use their wealth to keep at bay many of the misfortunes others suffer. Can these happy people be deceived?

In a tragic way Thomas says they are deceived; they have sold their hearts to what can never bring them lasting joy. Even though money and possessions are good and certainly necessary for human life, to think they constitute our most fitting good is a deadly illusion because they can never deliver the goodness that can bring us fully to life. Thomas's response to the claim that our ultimate joy is found in wealth is extremely blunt. He says that wealth cannot stand as our perfect good because it is less than we are; we will only be brought to fulness by something whose goodness surpasses us. What will make us happiest must be able to do great things for us. To be happy, Thomas reasons, is ultimately to possess the greatest possible good. If good things make us happy, then that which is best will bring us grandest joy. If we recall Thomas's point that our ultimate end is whatever finally quiets our desires, then our joy and happiness will reside in something so good that in possessing it our search for wholeness is over. It must be a good capable of bringing us to our fullest possible development, a good that stretches us, a good that consistently can carry us beyond previous levels of achievement and growth.

To think money can do this is preposterous. Our most lasting happiness resides in our most enduring wholeness. We shall find joy when we are one with whatever is most lovely and blessed. Can this possibly be money? Thomas argues that our happiness will be found in our ultimate end, and whatever that ultimate end is we are made for it, not it for us. We are to be turned toward it, we are to love and cherish it, we are to prize it as our most precious possession. Our ultimate end cannot be money, possessions, or any material thing simply because those things are made to help us, not rule us, and it is both silly and blasphemous to think we are made for them. This is why Thomas writes, "Man's happiness clearly cannot consist in natural riches. For they are sought for the sake of something else, namely the support of human life, and so are subordinate to its ultimate end, not the end itself. They are made for man, not man for them" (*ST*, I-II, 2,1).

Money is a means to an end, not the end itself. To turn money into our ultimate end is to take something less than us, and attempt to make it greater than us, even to make it our god. To worship at the altar of wealth is a sickening perversion of life, a cynical misunderstanding of who we are graced to be. To make wealth our god is invariably to diminish and destroy ourselves because the only way to find lasting joy in something less than us is by making ourselves even less than it. That is why the humanity of those who worship money eventually disappears. To make any lesser good our ultimate good is a most destructive perversion because it is to take something made for us and make it that for which we are made. That is why all misplaced loves are idolatrous, and why all idolatrous loves are deadly. In expending ourselves on lesser goods, we are destroyed.

The Inseparable Connection between Happiness and What Is Good

What then is the relationship between ourselves and whatever is going to make us happy? First, Thomas suggests that genuine happiness resides in whatever good is sought for its own sake, not for the sake of anything else. Happiness is being at one with the good beyond which there is no greater good; it is possessing the good every other good serves. There is one such perfect good, a blessed variety of intermediate goods. These other goods point to our most perfect good, and indeed their value is found in being the means by which our lasting good is gained.

Second, whatever will bring us perfect joy is not something less than us, but something so superior that in loving it we are brought to our optimum wholeness. Happiness is a matter of development, it is coming unto fulness through growing in excellence. We are perfected, not through something beneath us, but in something so gloriously blessed that it is out of our reach save through grace. Money is a good, but it is not perfectly good, for in no way does it have the excellence necessary for lasting joy. It has tremendous power to entice, but absolutely no power to redeem. It can lure us, entangle us, seduce us, but it cannot complete us, which is why if we love it most of all we are morally disfigured. Whatever will be our lasting happiness has a power not only to take us beyond ourselves, but to restore us. It has to have the power to heal, the power to grace and bless, the power to be perfectly life-giving and redeeming. Whatever will count for lasting joy has to have that excellence; otherwise, our lives will end not in bliss but despair. Whatever will bring us joy has to be capable of making us so much more than we already are. Money cannot do this. If we love it above all we have no respect for ourselves. To worship it is a cruel perversion of the human spirit, for wealth cannot make us more than we already are; it can only make us less.

Third, having said that money and possessions are not the greatest goods, Aquinas nonetheless insists they are necessary for life to be human at all. This tells us something about how he evaluates material things. As Jean Mouroux says in his book, *The Meaning of Man*, there ought to be but one absolute love, and that is God. "Let God be the first desired, the first sought, the first served, since He is not only the Source and the End, but also the God of Benediction."[1] If we are focused on God, Mouroux suggests, we glean well the true value of everything else because our love is proper. If we really do desire God most of all, then we shall know how to cherish everything else. The value of all the things in this world, including wealth and possessions, is that "in the hands of a rightful love"[2] they help us gain God. "Thus the Christian loves the temporal as something that shall help him to rejoin his God. His love is detached and freed from bondage because it goes first to God and to the eternal,"[3] Mouroux writes. The value in all these things is that they come from God to help us in our seeking of goodness and life, so they are to be cherished as gifts from God entrusted to us to enable the best possible life, which for Thomas is a life of love and worship of God. Our problems come when we sever the relationship between the good things of this world and the God from whom they came and to whom they are meant to direct us. This is why Mouroux is correct when he says, "The root of the mischief lies in the fact that temporal values have been severed from God. All come from God and are gifts of His love; all, therefore, should lead us to God and help us to achieve and fulfil our being by entering into union with God."[4]

Put differently, all the things of this earth, particularly material things, are not dangerous, but our love for them can be if we forget the purpose for which they are given. We can mold them into idols if we love them supremely instead of partially. It is not material things that are dangerous, but people of misdirected desires who are dangerous because they have yet to learn how to love all good things in a way proportionate to their goodness. By contrast, people who have charity—people who love God more than they love anything else— know rightly how to love all things because by keeping their love for God first they discern the true value of everything else. This is why Mouroux, following Aquinas, says:

> We may now easily perceive that what the Christian so emphatically condemns is not the love but the idolatry of the temporal. For this idolatry is a complete reversal of values, it changes their signification, and ends by falsifying temporal things along with man himself. It is a degradation. . . . He was made for the love of something higher than himself, and when temporal things usurp the first place in his affections then, inevitably, he falls beneath himself. . . . The violation of order brings its own reckoning: disorder felt in the bones, wholly crippling and destructive.[5]

Still, despite Aquinas's analysis, what are we to make of the fact that so many people live as if money were the best of all goods? Can so many people be wrong? Thomas says yes and his reasoning is straightforward: in morals, not all opinions are equal. There are a lot of silly ideas around because there are a lot of silly people, and anyone who thinks money is the best of all goods is patently foolish. "That money can do everything is the mass opinion of silly people who recognize only the material goods which can be bought," Thomas says. "To estimate human values, however, we should consult the wise, not the foolish, just as for matters gastronomical we go to those with well-educated tastes" (*ST,* I-II, 2,1). Aquinas will never conclude that happiness is what most people think it to be, or that what counts for joy can be determined by what has captured the majority's affections, because for him it is not where most people's affections lie that determines happiness, but happiness that determines what we must learn to be affectionate about.

Happiness is not a majority position; rather, happiness is understood by those who know what it means to be good. This is why Thomas says if we want to know the truth about happiness, or any other moral question, we should consult people who are wise and good, we should listen to people of virtue. Just as when we want to know what a delicious meal might be we consult a gourmet (and a hefty Thomas could appreciate this), so, too, if we want to know more about what is good and lovely we should turn to those in whom goodness truly shines. People who live as if money and things are the greatest possibility in life are silly, shallow people who do not know life at all. We should not listen to them because there is so little they really understand. In morals not all opinions are equal; the good have an authority the vicious do not and the reason is this: people who adore money are victims of misdirected loves, and in so disfiguring themselves they have lost all sense of who a human being is. They should be pitied, but they should never be heeded.

II. WHAT HAPPINESS IS AND WHERE IT IS TO BE FOUND

Thomas continues his investigation into various candidates for happiness. He asks whether happiness consists in fame and glory, whether it comes with honors, if it might be connected to power or physical skill, and if it has anything to do with pleasure. It is in examining each of these that he begins to build his own argument about where lasting beatitude is found. In what are we to be made perfectly happy? To answer this question, Thomas looks very carefully at who we are.

The first thing he notes is that men and women are not made for themselves (*ST,* I-II, 2,5). This is obvious, but it is important. We are not the purpose of our own existence. We are to live for the sake of something else. Aquinas's point is that we have life in order to be in relationship with something other than ourselves. We are not the greatest good, but we have life in order to find out what is and to love it. If we are not the purpose of our own existence, then we must search for what is. To be human, Aquinas suggests, is to be in love with this "something more." Put differently, we are not in virtue of ourselves, but in virtue of this something other, which is why we must search for it, learn to love it, and live forever in its presence. To know ourselves we must look elsewhere. If, as Thomas says, we are made not for ourselves but for something other, we must figure out what this something other is. All Aquinas suggests is that there is something vastly more important than ourselves in this world, and the most crucial project of the moral life is to find out what this something other is and to love it, for it is only in loving it that we can fully be. If we are made for something other than ourselves, then selfhood is a relationship with it. To be is to be in love with it. Mouroux captures well what Thomas means when he says about us, ". . . even to be itself it must needs seek something higher than itself,"[6] which is a fitting definition of a human being.

Thomas underscores the relational dimension of human existence. We cannot have life except through relationships with others and ultimately, to be sure, with God. Personhood is a social creation, not an individual one, inasmuch as we come to life through the crucible of friendship, through the love, care, and affection given us by others. The more fully we relate in love and trust to others, the more fully we come unto ourselves.[7] This is what Thomas means when he speaks of human existence as "participated" (*ST,* I-II, 2,5). We are in the measure that we participate in the lives of others; we have life to the degree that we live in communion with other people and with God. Our existence is not self-constituted, it is other-constituted; our self comes to us by participating in what is not ourself. Aquinas's point is that we do not have life when we stand apart, but when we stand in and from another. Isn't this why friendships are so important to us, and why we cannot think of ourselves apart from the people we love?

We cherish our friends, not only because they are good to us, but because we also know it is in and through them that we truly are ourselves. Our friends are indispensable because we have this heart-felt sense that we cannot be ourselves without them—and we are right. We know it is in relationship with our best friends that we become our best self.

Secondly, if existence is not solitary but relational, then life is more than sheer existence. Thomas touches this when he says that "mere existence is heightened by an additional value" (*ST,* I-II, 2,5). What he means is that life is more than simply existing. If we are made not for ourselves but for the sake of something other, then life is living in relationship with this something other, and we sense this. We know the purpose of life is not simply to live, but to be related to something more. We know that life has to be more than day-to-day survival, for simply surviving never satisfies us. If that is all our life is, then likely it is empty and sterile.

We want more than life, we want love in life. We want more than sheer existence, we want to love and to be loved, we want to cherish something more and we want to be cherished ourselves. We want to hold something good in our hearts and we want to be held there in love by another. We want to be in love with life, others, and God, and we want them all to love us. The "additional value" that heightens "mere existence" is love, specifically to love and to be loved by the good that is our happiness. Life is more than existence; it is being in love with the greatest of all goods, it is friendship with that good, it is intimacy with that good, it is communion with that good. This is why Thomas says, "Manifestly man is destined to an end beyond himself, for he himself is not the supreme good. And therefore the final goal . . . cannot just be his own continuance" (*ST,* I-II, 2,5). We are not given life simply to exist, but to love and to be loved, to grow in that love, to be changed by it, to be freed by it, to find joy in it. This is why we can be busy and still feel haunted by loneliness and sadness. This is why we can look at our lives and say there is much good about it, but something vital seems to be missing. When we feel this we are searching for the something more, and when we sense this we are being called to deeper possibilities of love.

Third, and not surprisingly, Thomas says authentic happiness is connected to goodness. The only genuinely happy people are the virtuous. We may flinch at this, but Thomas will not be budged. When he says, "Virtue's true reward is happiness itself" (*ST,* I-II, 2,2), he is following Aristotle's conclusion that happiness is not something other than the virtues, but *is* the virtuous life. Happiness is being good, it is participating in goodness and growing in goodness. For Aquinas, to be virtuous is to be happy, which is why we cannot find joy and peace until we become truly good, and it is also why the deeper our sharing in goodness, the happier we shall become. For Thomas, happiness is not natural, but is acquired and developed. Happiness comes through a certain way of life, a virtuous way of life. Moreover, happiness is doing certain things, namely doing good things. Thomas sees happiness not so much as a feeling, though it is partly that, but more as an activity, as living a certain way. Happiness is being virtuous, it is doing good and becoming good, it is love being practiced. Happiness is doing whatever will bring us to our fullest and most genuine development. It is our most proper and distinctive function, which is why we can say happiness is the best thing we can do.

Genuine happiness cannot be found in evil people, it can never be had through wickedness. Evil may bring pleasure, but it can never bring happiness because "happiness is complete well-being and incompatible with any evil" (*ST,* I-II, 2,4). Thomas grants that wickedness may thrive and evil people may often prosper, but they cannot be genuinely happy because they are involved in a deterioration of themselves. Wickedness brings decay, not life; it does not restore, it perverts. If happiness is being brought to the fullness of our most proper development, then we will be truly happy in the measure that we achieve our grandest possibility and share in our most promising good. This is why Thomas insists beatitude is not compatible with evil. Evil turns us away from life, it disfigures, it makes us morally ugly, while goodness is life and is beautiful and is freeing. To be happy is to live in and from the most beautiful good, it is even to grow in the likeness of this good, which is why, as we shall see, Thomas eventually insists that our happiness is friendship with God. If happiness is commensurate with goodness, then the greatest joy is in proportion to the greatest goodness. It is because of this that Thomas says our growth in happiness hinges on our growth in the goodness of God. This is why he also concludes that happiness is holiness, and that being godly is requisite for joy. Thomas hints this when he says, "There is a drive within all things towards some likeness to God, who is their first beginning and final end" (*ST,* I-II, 2,4). But he captures it even more fittingly when he writes, "Therefore to show some reflection of God by their power does not approach to happiness, unless they [human beings] also become like God in goodness" (*ST,* I-II, 2,4). This is Thomas's most succinct definition of happiness: happiness is becoming like God in goodness.

Why Happiness Is a Quality of Soul

There is one obvious objection to this. Good people do not always seem happy. Their goodness does not protect them from adversity. They, too, are burdened with life's misfortunes, they, too, are often visited by bad luck; in fact, in many respects it seems good people suffer more, they may even suffer because they are good. The lives of the saints attest to this. They knew tragedy, in many respects their lives seem to have been an endless chronicle of being tested by adversity. How then can Thomas claim that the virtuous are the only genuinely happy ones?

Because he argues that happiness is not a mood or a feeling, but quality of soul. Here is how he reasons. He agrees that happiness is something outside us, if we are speaking about the object of happiness. He has already said that in order to be happy we must be related to what is good, and in order to know perfect happiness we must love the perfectly good. But then he added that our happiness grows insofar as we come to possess this good ourselves. By loving the good we begin to take on its quality, and it becomes part of us, an aspect of our being. We possess it internally because we have been formed in its likeness. What makes us happy is outside us in the sense that it stands apart from us, but we become happy when through love we have made it part of ourselves.

We are talking about intimacy, but about the most radical and enduring intimacy of all, the intimacy of likeness to what we most desire. We can see this in friendships when each absorbs something of the other's goodness. We can see it in marriages when a husband has been changed by the loveliness of his wife. We can see it in all those relationships in which we begin to take on aspects of the ones we love. Through love we become part of the other's being and they become part of ours. We have union by passing over into the other's self. Thomas makes this point about happiness when he says happiness is laying hold of our good, but laying hold of it internally. Happiness is being united with our good, but it is a union of likeness, a kinship of similarity. To be happy is to have taken within ourselves our beloved, it is to have absorbed within our souls the goodness we endlessly seek. This is why Thomas says happiness is being "conjoined in any way with the thing on which we set our heart." As he elaborates:

If, however, by this we refer to the gaining or possessing, or to our being conjoined in any way with the thing on which we set our heart, then our ultimate end [happiness] implies something within us and on the part of our soul, for it is then that we come to happiness. To sum up: the thing itself desired as the final end is that which gives substance to happiness and makes a person happy, though happiness itself is defined by the holding of it. The conclusion to be drawn is that happiness is a real condition of soul, yet is founded on a thing outside the soul. (*ST,* I-II, 2,7)

We can understand what Thomas means if we reflect on who strike us as happy people. What are happy people like? What do we sense when we are with them? Their happiness seems to rise from within them. In a sense, they are their happiness because it is hard to separate the joy and peace we feel in their presence from who they are. We do not think of their happiness as one aspect of who they are; rather, we think of them as happy in themselves. Their happiness is neither peripheral nor superficial, but is a personal trait, a dimension of their character. And we sense they are happy because they are one with what they love. There is little discrepancy in them between what they seek and what they possess. Happiness is holding to what we love, insofar as it is no longer something apart from us, but something whose likeness we share, and that is how these people seem to us. By loving something good for so long they have become like it. Every love brings likeness, and their love has brought likeness to something eminently and refreshingly good. By loving it, they have been transformed from within. They truly have been converted because the goodness and beauty of what they love has become transparent in themselves.

Perfect happiness is perfect assimilation with the best of all goods. As we shall see, Thomas says that happiness is the ultimate effect of what we love on who we are, inasmuch as loving something good and beautiful for a lifetime makes us rich in that same goodness and beauty. We absorb the preciousness of what we love, we take on its goodness, which is why we are happy; what we have sought for so long as our joy we possess, not in some transient, fickle way, but as an enduring quality of soul. We can say we are happiness not in the sense that everything always goes our way or that we are perpetually cheerful, but in the sense that we have absorbed the effects of our love. To be happy is to hold what we love, and for Aquinas we hold it in the most personal, enduring way possible: we are conformed to its goodness.

Why Perfect Happiness Is Found in God

Still, because happiness comes in the perfect assimilation of ourself into the most perfecting good, it is not something we have all at once. Happiness is gradually, sometimes painstakingly, attained. It is the work of a virtuous lifetime. We cultivate joy as we cultivate goodness. This is why we can say happiness increases with the ongoing and never-ending remaking of ourselves. Happiness is conversion because to be happy is to have been converted into the goodness of God. Happiness is surrender, because to be happy is to have handed ourselves over to the love that can do immeasurably more for us than we could ever do for ourselves. To be happy is to be transfigured in holiness, to shine with the goodness of God, but because God's goodness always infinitely surpasses us, our happiness can forever increase. Heaven may have to be everlasting because there is no limit to the happiness God's goodness can bring.

We know where Aquinas's argument is taking us. When all is said and done, our happiness lies not in any created good, but in the perfect, everlasting goodness of God. To be happy is to be united with what is most lovely and blessed; it is communion with pure goodness. Thomas has said from the start that our happiness is realized in whatever brings us to our fullest and most fitting development, and now he identifies this as God, for God can do more for us than anything else. In God is a goodness that can bless us eternally, a goodness that can continue to change us and enrich us. In God alone is the goodness that brings fulness of life, that is why God is our happiness and joy. Every other good contributes to life, but is not life. Every other good leaves us desiring more. We taste these goods but we continue to search; we possess them but we are driven by longing; we have them and we still are lonely. The incompleteness of every other good points us to a better good. To be happy, Thomas says, we must know complete fulfillment and be lacking in nothing, but when we have wealth, honor, fame, power, reputation, and pleasure, as good and as necessary as all these things are, we know we are still lacking that something more that alone can draw us to wholeness. Only in God resides a good blessed enough to heal and redeem, which is why God is our ultimate good and the fulness of our joy.

But Thomas has a problem. He knows there remains one objection to his claim that God is our perfect happiness and our absolutely fulfilling good. The problem is this: how can we who are not God ever possess God in a way to know such lasting joy? How can we who are so different from God, limited, finite, and earthly, enjoy the splendid goodness of One who seems everything we are not? Granted we may desire God more than we desire anything else, but this does not mean we necessarily have a capacity for a relationship with God. Can the infinite, perfect good be the happiness of those who are creaturely and finite? Or do we simply, if tragically, remain worlds apart? If so, then those who argue that happiness is found not in God but in something of this earth are right, they are the realists. If so, people who seek their joy in wealth, fame, honor, power, and prestige have accepted who we are, creatures who cannot reach out to more good than the goods of this world.

Thomas grants the force of this claim. He knows there is no apparent reason we should believe that human beings who are so radically other than God can be united with God. In raising this point Thomas is not questioning God, but is questioning our capacity for God. Can we find joy in One so different from ourselves? Are we capable of relating to the God Thomas says is our only possible lasting joy? If God is to be our happiness we must have some capacity to be in relationship with God and truly love God. Otherwise, no matter how much Thomas might want to disagree, whatever happiness is possible for us must come through the things of this world. This is how Thomas poses the problem:

> Again, man is made happy by an object which brings to rest his natural desire. This, however, does not reach out to more good than it can hold. Since he has not the capacity for a good beyond the bounds of all creation, it would seem that he can become happy through some created good, and here he finds his happiness (*ST,* I-II, 2,8).

Is seeking our happiness in God "reaching out to more good than we can hold"? Thomas says this point would be insurmountable if there were no way we could have a relationship with God. If God remains infinitely apart from us, God cannot be our happiness and joy; however, there are two reasons we can believe otherwise. First, there is grace. Grace is the gift of God's love which enables us to enjoy God in a way that otherwise would be impossible. It is through grace, which is always pure gift, that we are made capable of relationship with God. Grace, in Aquinas's language, "elevates" us so we can seek God, love God, and have communion with God. It is through God, and not ourselves, that this is made possible for us; the gift of God's love empowers us to love in return.

Second, if grace comes from God's side, desire comes from ours. Thomas grants that if we were finite in every way God could not be our joy, for we cannot "reach out to more good" than we can hold. But there is, he contends, one way we are not finite: we have unlimited desire. We are limited in every way but one—we have unlimited desire, unlimited longing. Our desire is the one thing about us that is not restricted and we know this. We feel the ongoing hunger for something infinitely good, we are stalked by the longing for something perfectly blessed and precious. Though we are limited, we want unlimited good, though we are restricted, we want to love unrestrictedly. This is why we can never settle with created goods; they are too limited and restrictive for the boundlessness of our spirit. And so we keep searching for more, we continue to move to what seems forever beyond us because we know nothing less will satisfy us, nothing less will bring us peace. This is why Thomas says we "can reach out to the infinite" (*ST,* I-II, 2,8). We seek the infinite through the openness of desire, and only something indefectibly good will satisfy this desire. "For man to rest content with any created good is not possible," Thomas writes, "for he can be happy only with complete good which satisfies his desire altogether: he would not have reached his ultimate end were there something still remaining to be desired" (*ST,* I-II, 2,8).

We shall never find lasting joy if we remain restless of heart. We seek the good which heals our restlessness, and that is what joy is—it is longing, searching, hungering, desiring come to rest. For Thomas such peace is found only in God. God is our happiness because in God we want no more. God is our happiness because in God we find the joy we have always relentlessly sought. We seek, Thomas says, "the good without reserve," that alone will satisfy us, and such good "is found not in anything created, but in God alone" (*ST,* I-II, 2,8).

In this chapter we have considered the one thing everyone wants. We have spoken about happiness. We have said much about what happiness is not, but we have also reflected on what happiness is. To be happy is to be satisfied, but it is also to be made whole. It is to be content, but it is also to be perfected. To be happy is to be good and to be holy. Happiness is joy, but joy comes when we desire no more, when our searching has ended because we have found peace. After looking at all the ways we try to find happiness, Thomas urges us to look to God. There are many good things, but only God is perfectly good. God is our final, most perfect, and everlasting happiness because in God alone lives the goodness that heals, redeems and restores.

To be with God is to be happy, but Thomas understands this in a very particular way. We are happy when we have intimacy with God. We have found joy when we are so much a part of God's life that God and we are one. Thomas calls this happiness friendship. It is how he understands charity. Charity is friendship with God. It is an astonishing claim to say we can be friends of God. What Thomas means by it is what we shall next explore.

4. Charity: The Virtue of Friendship with God

Hidden away in the *Summa* is an astonishing claim. Thomas says we can be friends of God. It sounds marvelous but farfetched. How can we speak of God in terms we reserve for the best relationships of our lives? Can we have the same intimacy, the same endearing kinship, the same heartfelt joy with God that we know with our closest friends? Thomas says we can; in fact, he says to speak of our relationship with God in any other way is to misunderstand how God wants to know and love us. God wants to love us as friend, God wants an intimacy with us that is personal and deep, God wants to abide in our lives as keenly as possible, loving us, cherishing us, doing everything for our good. We can think of other relationships of our lives as friendships, but we are not accustomed to thinking this way of God. We know God loves us, but God can seem too infinitely beyond us to be our friend. We know God wants what is best for us, but to speak of our relationship with God as friendship seems too fantastic to be true.

But Thomas says it is true. He speaks of charity as friendship with God, a friendship which is "begun here in this life by grace, but will be perfected in the future life by glory" (*ST,* I-II, 65,5). This is Thomas's vision of the moral life. We who are children of God are called to be the friends of God. We are to love God not just in any way, but in friendship. It seems almost blasphemous to think of God this personally and intimately, but for Thomas it is the bedrock claim of the Christian moral life. He believes the unbelievable: we are called to an ever-deepening friendship with the God who is our happiness, a friendship of love given and love received, a friendship in which each seeks the good of the other, and through love finally become one. Friendship with God is the vocation all share, absolutely the only thing that must happen to us if we are to know the happiness God wants for us. Our life can be friendship with God. Thomas calls this friendship charity, and it is the love guiding and empowering his vision of the moral life. It is an ethic of love, but specifically the beautiful, astounding love of charity. It is an ethic of relationship, but the core relationship for Thomas is a friendship with God that captures the most profoundly promising possibility of our lives. We are called through love to be for God who God has always been for us, a friend, a source of happiness and delight, one who is key to the other person's joy.

Who are we? We are children of God called through love to become God's friends. We are people dear to God, people important to God, people extraordinarily precious to God. Who are we? We are people God desires, people God longs to be with, people whose lives God so deeply wants to share, not in any kind of intimacy, but in the heartfelt intimacy of friendship. Who are we? We are people called to want with God what God always wants with us, a life together, a kinship of hearts, an ever-deepening union of love. To become for God what God has always been for us is the moral life's goal for Thomas. We are to accept the offer of God's friendship and grow in it. We are summoned to charity, not only because there is no more demanding love, but also because in that transformation of ourselves unto God we become enough like God to be able to share the happiness of God. That is what God has always wanted for us, and that is why God calls us to divine friendship.

It is an astonishing claim, an almost blasphemous claim, to think we can be God's friends. At first glance it seems impossible, a fullness too good to be true; and yet, such an enchanting possibility—a possibility whose strangeness never leaves us—is for Aquinas what God wants every human life to achieve. Charity is friendship with God, and it is the love we are called to practice because it is the love that will bring us never-ending joy. A hauntingly beautiful possibility charity is, and in this chapter we shall explore what such friendship means by looking at Thomas's treatment of it in I-II, 65, 5 and II-II, 23, 1 of the *Summa Theologiae.*

I. WHAT IT MEANS TO SPEAK
OF GOD AS FRIEND

All friendship is love, but not all love is friendship. Friendship is a special kind of love. This is why when Thomas says "charity signifies not only the love of God, but also a certain friendship with him" (*ST,* I-II, 65,5), he has in mind a distinctive relationship between God and ourselves. We are not simply called to love God, we are to love God as friend. To be God's friend is to shape and express our love a certain way. To have charity is to make our love life with God conform to the qualities characteristic of friendship. A friendship is more than a relationship of closeness or good feeling. It is a relationship marked by three characteristics.

The first is benevolence. If we are somebody's friend we seek their good and work for their well-being. To be someone's friend is to want what is best for them and to delight when they have it. There is an energy to friendship, and it is the energy of friends actively and joyously working for one another's good. This is what makes a relationship a friendship—it is wanting what is genuinely good for our friend. We can sense this in the good friendships of our lives. We know who our friends are by how they stand to us and what they want for us. They do not attempt to use us or manipulate us; they are not interested in us only for the sake of what we can do for them, and if they are it does not take long to discover they are not our friends. We know our friends in this way. They are concerned for us. We trust them because we know they want what is best for us. They protect us by always seeking our good, they challenge us by calling us to our best self. We may know lots of people in our life, but we may have preciously few good friends precisely because of the kind of person friendship requires. Friendship demands a person of such generous spirit that he or she really will find joy in our good. If someone is our friend we are more than an aspect of some plan they might have; rather, we are someone who means so much to them that they find purpose and meaning in life by doing good for us.

This is why Thomas says benevolence is not only wishing our friends well, but actively working for their well-being. Friendship is an activity, but it is expressly the activity of each working for the other's good. That is the life of a friendship, a friendship's heart and soul. A good friend seeks our good, and does this because she or he loves us. The life of any good friendship is this active, genuine working for the good of the friend. For us to be anyone's friend is to be for them, it is to understand the task and purpose of the friendship to be a seeking and enabling of the friend's happiness. This is what it means to be benevolent to another. As the word suggests, it is to wish nothing but the best for them. Good friends are this way toward us. They not only work for our good, but we can even say that our good is their good, and that the joy of the friendship for them is the chance to do something fine for the person they love. This is why they are delighted when they see us flourishing.

Friendship reverses the direction of love's concern. In friendship the good sought is not immediately our own, but the friend's. There is a penchant to friendship, an overriding concern. Its love interest is the happiness and well-being of the friend. The strategy of true friendship is to discover one's good, not by directly seeking it, but by devoting oneself to the good of the other. In this way, our good is the friend's good, our happiness is seeking the happiness of the friend. We know that to be a good friend is to want the good of the friend. Through practicing such generosity we discover that the friend's good truly is our good, and that we are happiest when we are devoting ourselves to what is best for them.

This is what is different about friendship love. All love shares a desire for a particular good, but what distinguishes loves is the one for whom the good is desired and the reason it is desired. Friendship is the love whose whole thrust and energy toils for the good of the other. It is a love whose very activity is to cultivate the well-being and flourishing of the other, not because the one who loves has no good of his own, but because what he loves and sees as his good is the good of his friend. Benevolence implies not only that the friend is loved for herself, but also because she is loved the active seeking of her good is the sustaining project of the friend's life. To love with the benevolence proper to friendship means not only that one hopes for the good of the other, but also that one consecrates his energy to seeking and upholding her good. That is what friendship is—devotion to the good of the one we love.

What It Means to Have Benevolence for God

But what does this mean when the friend in mind is God? How do we practice benevolence to God? Put differently, does it make any sense to wish God well? A story may help. *An Interrupted Life* is the diary of Etty Hillesum, a young Jewish woman who lived in Amsterdam during the years of World War II and eventually met death in Auschwitz. In the latter months of her life, it becomes clear to Etty that she and so many other Jewish people will die at the hands of the Nazis and there is little God can do to help them; however, Etty does not conclude there is nothing she can do to help God. She vows to come to God's assistance even if God cannot come to hers. She figures if God is powerless to save her from death, this does not mean she is powerless to look after God. That is what Etty does. She resolves, in the face of God's helplessness, to look after God's interests in the world. She promises to live whatever life remains for her in seeking what is best for God. Though Etty does not use this language, in Aquinas's sense she is truly a friend of God. As she writes one day in her diary,

> But one thing is becoming increasingly clear to me: that You cannot help us, that we must help You to help ourselves. And that is all we can manage these days and also all that really matters: that we safeguard that little piece of You, God, in ourselves. And perhaps in others as well. Alas, there doesn't seem to be much You Yourself can do about our circumstances, about our lives. Neither do I hold You responsible. You cannot help us but we must help You and defend Your dwelling place inside us to the last.[1]

Etty practices benevolence to God and discovers something wonderful about the deepest possibilities of human action. She learns that a God who is powerless gains power through people like her who live to protect God's interests in the world. Though it may sound outlandish, Etty befriends God and in that act of befriending gains a remarkable insight about the potential we have for goodness. Sometimes in our world we may have a power God lacks. This sounds farfetched, but it is an implication of friendship. Just as God so often intercedes in our lives, helping us, blessing us, befriending us, so, too, can we sometimes intercede for God by watching after God's interests in the world. God always has benevolence toward us, but there is absolutely no reason we cannot have benevolence toward God. That is part of every friendship, watching after one another, protecting one another, helping one another, and we are wrong if we think it is all one-sided. It is not true that only we need God's friendship, for there is a way, Etty learns, that God needs our friendship too. God depends on our good to do good in the world, God counts on us to help carry through God's purposes. Friends need one another and help one another, and we, too, can help God in the world by always seeking and practicing what God wants. As *An Interrupted Life* makes clear, an otherwise powerless God gains power through Etty's resolution to be good; an otherwise frustrated God is liberated through people like Etty who vow to live in a way that makes things better for God. Our ultimate nobility is to safeguard God's interests in the world, but it is also what it means to be a good friend of God. To be God's friend is to watch after God in the world, it is to be benevolent to God. Etty practices grand benevolence when she assures God that she will watch after God in the world. Friends are like that—they look after one another, they stand by one another, they help seek one another's good. God is always that way with us, but if friendship thrives between us then we must be that way with God. We have benevolence toward God when, like Etty, we try to make God's will our own.

Friendship Is Mutuality in Love

And yet, there must be something more to friendship than benevolence. The devotion benevolence entails, if it is not shared, can be frustrating and deadening. There is nothing sadder than to love and be devoted to one who shows no affection or concern for us. It hurts when someone we want to befriend offers no return to our friendship. We have had the experience of channeling our energies to seeking the good for someone we love without ever having that affection reciprocated. It hurts and disappoints us because we know despite our wishes that person is not our friend. We may want to befriend him, but his refusal to embrace our benevolence with the offer of his own signals that he may be a recipient of our charity, but is hardly our friend. This is why Thomas says the benevolence of friendship must be mutual. Simply wishing another well does not a friendship make. It is necessary for friendship, but not sufficient. To be friendship, the good we wish for another must also be wished for us. This is the second mark of friendship: its love and benevolence must be mutual, a love in which each person knows the well-wishing she offers the other is returned by him to her. As Aquinas says, "Yet good will alone is not enough for friendship for this requires mutual loving; it is only with a friend that a friend is friendly" (*ST,* II-II, 23,1).

Friendships cannot be one-sided. Friendships are relationships in which each person is committed to the other. No more than one person can make a marriage work, a friendship, too, demands the pledge of both to the other's well-being. We may love someone dearly and give ourself to seeking her good, but unless our love is returned its status is kindness, not friendship. Friendships are two-sided, they are relationships in which each person knows the good he wishes the other is also wished for him. Friendship is a partnership in care and affection, it is a society of love in which each works for the best of the other. We know this. We know who our friends are and who are not. We may be good to many, but our friends are those who are likewise good to us. We sense who our true friends are. We can count on them. We have experienced their goodness. We feel their dedication. We have been enriched by them. What comes through is how much they desire our good. This is why we can speak of friendships as communities of affection in which two bound in love work to make that love the possession of the other. Benevolence is obviously part of this, but it is not enough for friendship. To be friendship, the good we want for another has to be shared consciously and intentionally by the friends. Friends must know they are friends, they must be aware of one another's benevolence; they have to have the confidence that each is truly for the other. We can sense the importance of reciprocity for friendship when we consider those times the love we offered was never returned. There remains an incompleteness to love that is not met by love. Friendships live when love meets love, where one gift of love kisses another. Friends are those who recognize each other's love, share it and rejoice in it. Robert Johann puts this well:

> For friendship, it is not sufficient to love another directly as myself; to be friendship, my love of benevolence must be explicitly reciprocated. Friendship exists only between those who love one another. Thus it is conceived as adding to a one-sided love of benevolence a certain society of lover and beloved in their love.[2]

Why Good Friends Make Us Good People

Johann's description of friendship as a "certain society," a miniature community of sorts, in which love and goodness are exchanged, reminds us that friendships are a way of life that teach us what it means to be good and actually make us good. We may not be accustomed to think of friendships this way, but good friendships are schools of virtue. It is what happens between friends who are good that actually makes us grow in goodness, and is the moral beauty of a good friendship. We enjoy them, but we also grow through them, shining in a goodness we otherwise could not receive. Good friends make us better people. We are indebted to our friends because we know we are better for having known them. But why? Because every friendship is a relationship through which loving and doing good to another makes us better persons. Friendships are schools of virtue because in them we learn well how to practice the good, particularly justice. Our friends not only give us opportunities to do good, they challenge us in goodness, they stretch us to deeper levels of moral achievement, they will never let us be satisfied with a goodness already attained. Friends are those who agree on what is important, and if what is important is a mutual desire to grow in goodness, then that is exactly what the friendship will achieve. Every friendship is forged around some good that brings the friends together, and the life of the friendship is to nurture one another from the good both want to embody.

This is one reason we spend time with our friends. We spend time with them because we enjoy being with them—their company is a delight to us—but also because we sense we cannot be ourselves without them. Friendships constitute our lives. So much of who we are is what our friendships have made of us. We can even say we are our friendships, at least in the sense that it is through them that much of our identity is formed. Friends are those who, through their loving attention to us, sculpt us to wholeness. They practice their love on us, and thus bring us into being in a way we could never have accomplished ourselves. Friends see things in us we could never see ourselves, or even if we do see it they alone know how to draw it out of us. A good friend is someone who draws the best out of us, someone who creates us in the most promising way. That is why a good friend is something like an artist. Through the ingenuity of their love they shape us in goodness and beauty, they make us someone splendid.

In her novel, *Rough Strife,* Lynne Sharon Schwartz tells the story of the marriage of Ivan and Caroline. One day Caroline reminisces about time they spent together in Florence, and she recalls the statues of Michelangelo. The beauty of those statues first hidden away in uncarved blocks of marble becomes, for Caroline, a metaphor of their marriage. "She thought often about Michelangelo's statues that they had seen years ago in Florence in the first excitement of their love, figures hidden in the block of stone, uncovered only by the artist's chipping away the excess, the superficial blur, till smooth and spare, the true shape is revealed. She and Ivan were hammer and chisel to each other."[3] So are our friends to us. Through their love good friends chip away at the excess until our "true shape is revealed." Friends are "hammer and chisel" to one another because through their love they bring each other more gloriously to life.

If we consider any of the good friendships of our lives we ought to have a sense that we are better because of them. Friendships ought to be ennobling. We should grow through them to greatness. There are some people we appreciate because we can be our best self with them. If we look back over the history of the friendship we can see how their love has changed us. We are not now the people we were before meeting them; we are, happily, significantly better. What is it that good friends do that helps us become good? It may be that they put us in touch with what we cherish most. We said already that every friendship comes to life around whatever good the friends share. This can be quite varied. Friends come together around baseball or horseback riding or card playing or sewing. But they also gather because they love what is good. There are all kinds of friendships, but the best friendships are those joined by a mutual love for virtue, and ultimately a mutual love for God. Why do we seek these friendships? Because we rightly think we cannot become good without them. Friends need to spend time together in order to remain friends, but they also need to spend time together in order to share the good of their friendship. There is no other way to touch some goods than in company with those who share them. Friendship is a society or community constituted by those who agree on a good they seek, and it is through the life of the friendship that the good they seek is mediated through the love they share. We need to spend time with our friends because it is through them that we are endowed with what we love, whether that be card playing, reading poetry together, or growing in virtue. In this sense friendship is a moral reality, and perhaps the constitutive moral activity of our lives, because through it we receive from another the good we most devotedly love.

Friendship's rationale is to be the community in which the ongoing formation of the friends in virtue takes place. And what friendship teaches us is that the good in which we see ourselves completed is not something we can offer ourselves, but is only something we can receive from a friend whose love continually bestows it. Virtue friendships are based on a good we need in order to grow in excellence, but it is only a good we can receive. We cannot reach this good through ourselves; we can only reach it through the friend who offers it. We touch the good in the crucible of friendship in which each gives to the other the good both desire, but could never reach alone. We come in touch with our good through our friends, which is one reason why we spend time with them. We reach what we desire through our friends, who are the ones whose love forms us in the good we hope to become. This is why to have a good friend is to be tutored in virtue. Good friends make us good because the life of the friendship is a sharing and delighting in what is excellent, noble, and beautiful. We know there are some people with whom we can fully be ourselves, and these are the people, hopefully, who call forth what is best in us. If they are, then it is with them that we grow in goodness and virtue, and it is through them that the most promising features of ourselves are unveiled. Good friendships are schools of virtue because by being with people who are good and want to be good, we learn what true goodness is and grow in it ourselves. This is also why we are so indebted to our friends; we realize we could never have become good without them.

How Friendship with God Brings Us Most Fully to Life

If this is true for our good friends, it is eminently true in our friendship with God. It is through the mutuality of friendship that friends grow in goodness, each offering to the other the love and virtue both seek. Something similar happens in charity-friendship with God. There is an exchange of love there, a reciprocity, in which we seek what is in the best interest of God and God seeks what is most fulsome for ourselves. Friends work together for one another's good; that is the mutuality of friendship, the give-and-take that is friendship's heart and soul. The activity of friendship is this shared upbuilding in goodness. This is how Aquinas understood our friendship with God. He argued that if every good friendship is a relationship we have with those whose love completes us, then this is all the more true with God. In his *Commentary on the Sentences of Peter Lombard,* Thomas speaks of friendship as a certain society of lover and beloved in love, and then refers specifically to charity as a friendship we have with God in which God loves us and we love God, this mutual exchange of love effecting a society or partnership in love between God and ourselves.[4]

What is going on in this friendship with God? From our side, to seek God's good is to want to do God's will. It is to adore and praise and worship God, to delight in God's goodness and to find joy in God's love. It is to serve God because we are grateful, to be for God because we love. By doing all these things, prayer, worship, service, love, adoration, we enhance God by glorifying God, we enrich God by giving God life. But God does something for us as well. For God to seek our good is for God to want what is best for us. If God loves us God wants what is best for us, and this is nothing more than to have fulness of life in God by becoming like God. For God to work for our good through love is for God to draw us ever more fully into the Divine Love. We said before that good friendships make us good because through that exchange of love we are brought more fully to life. We spoke of friends seeing possibilities for goodness and life in us we could only dimly perceive. We said a good friend is like an artist, and under the artistry of their love they sculpt us to life. But what artistry can match the beauty of God's love? God is the master artist of love, befriending us in a way that calls forth our most blessed self. God sees our fullest potential—our redeemed and holy self—and God loves us in a way that beckons this self to life. God's love works on us too, redeeming us, restoring us, healing us, ever creating us anew. God sees what is most graced about us hidden away under so much that is false and destructive and, like Caroline and Ivan in *Rough Strife,* through the artistry of his love, God chips "away the excess, the superficial blur, till smooth and spare, the true shape is revealed." God is "hammer and chisel" to each one of us.

Too, just as in our other friendships we are put in touch with our good, in charity-friendship with God we are put in touch with the divine goodness. God is our ultimate joy, the One in whom we find happiness and peace, but God is a good we can reach not directly, but through our friendship with God. It is God who puts us in touch with God's goodness, God who brings to us fulness of life. God is the One in whom we are completed, but such fulsome restoration is not something we can offer ourselves, it is only a gift we can receive. This gift offered and received is the heartbeat of charity. Every friendship thrives on what is offered and exchanged, and charity thrives on the offer of God's life and happiness to us. If God is our friend, God wants what is best for us, and what is best for us is the Divine Life, the fulness of life, joy, peace, and happiness that is God. It is exactly this that God brings to us in charity. This offer of life takes root in "the love of God . . . poured out in our hearts through the Holy Spirit" (Rom 5:5), it grows through charity, and it is perfected when the Spirit of Love is wholly alive in us. This is the friendship begun in grace and perfected in glory, and it is something God continually offers us. As God loves us God calls us to life, not any kind of life, but life in God. As God loves us, God offers us good, not any kind of good, but the goodness of God. As God loves us, God wants us to be happy, to enjoy not any kind of happiness, but to share the very happiness of God. This is God's benevolence, this is what it means for God to want what is best for us. A perfect lover, God offers us perfect joy.

Aquinas sometimes speaks of friendships as "conversations" in the good. The life together of the friends is an ongoing conversation in the good both seek. To have a friendship is to be turned to something good; in fact, it is some good that constitutes and identifies the friendship. Friendships are known through whatever shared good brings them to life. Friends know the good they share and they know the point of their friendship is to allow one another to participate in that good more completely; they understand their friendship to be a conversing in this good. This conversation in the good of the friendship makes possible the conversion to the good the friendship intends.

When Thomas speaks of friendship this way, he has charity in mind. The friendship we have with God must be understood as a never-ending conversation with God about the good integral to charity.[5] But as the word "conversation" suggests, to converse in the good of charity is to be changed by it. Like any friendship, charity-friendship with God is a way of being a self, but more exactly of becoming a self. The more we are turned to the good of charity, which is the splendid goodness of God, the more we are transfigured. The "conversation" in the good of charity is the conversion of ourselves to God. To be converted is to be turned into something more than we already are. Charity-friendship with God is a life of ongoing conversion because we cannot suffer such love without being changed by it, and that is exactly our hope. We want to be changed. We want to become something better. Charity offers the most radical conversion because God's love promises the most beautiful good. Every love changes us, but no love changes us so thoroughly and hopefully as God's love does. Charity is a life of conversion because to live in friendship with God is to be remade by the goodness of God.

To be God's friend is to give God freedom to do with us what God wants, it is to open our lives to God so unflinchingly that God can shape us as perfect love sees fit. That is the work of charity's love, sculpting us in the goodness of God, shaping us in the beauty of holiness. Charity is the lifelong conversion of ourselves to God. Every love brings likeness because to love is to take on the quality of what is loved. Charity brings likeness to God because when we love God and let God love us, we are formed in the Spirit of Love, we are changed in the goodness of God. Every love changes us, but only charity changes us unto God. And that is our hope, because if we could not share God's goodness we could never know the peace, joy, and love that alone brings rest to our desire. Charity's promise is exactly our hope: we cannot love God and remain the same. No one who is a friend of God remains the same, and that is reassuring, because it is a sign that we do not hope for goodness in vain. In charity we become exactly who we need to become to find joy; we begin to hint of holiness.

How Charity Brings Likeness to God

In Book Three of his *Summa Contra Gentiles,* Thomas says "the ultimate end of things is to become like God," and this happens insofar as "created things . . . attain to divine goodness."[6] The strategy of charity is to bring us a likeness to God deep enough that we are able to enjoy the happiness God enjoys. Every love brings likeness, and charity brings a likeness to God which enables us to be a friend of God. To be someone's friend is to be "another self" to them, to be so like them not only in tastes and interests, but in character, goodness and virtue, that they come to look upon us as a reflection of themselves. The third mark of friendship is that through the love that bonds the friends, each becomes "another self" for the other. This is akin to Aristotle's idea that the friend is like a mirror for us. We can see ourselves in them because we know we too have been formed, shaped, and defined by the same love. They are like ourselves because through the friendship they have come to embody the same good. We know this is true with our friends. They give us a sense of who we are inasmuch as they are a reflection of what we, too, consider good, precious and lovely. They are not identical to us, but they are like us in what they value and consider important, they are people of similar vision and ideals, this is why we can speak of them as another self to us.

The same is true when our friend is God. We cannot love God and remain unchanged. To love God in charity is to become like God in goodness. There is a terrible vulnerability to any love because to love is to become like the one we love. There is a loss of control in this, indeed a loss of self, because to love is to lose one kind of self and take on another. Nowhere is this transformation more drastic than in charity. Charity fosters vulnerability to God, an openness so exhaustive that we ultimately become defenseless before the love who is our life. To become defenseless before God in charity is to absorb fully the Spirit, it is to be made over by the love that is God's happiness, and when that transfiguration is achieved we have not only changed, we have changed in a way that makes us enough like God to be another self to God; it is then we can truly speak of ourselves as God's friends. We can speak of God as another self to us at least in the sense that we want what God wants, that God's will is our delight, that we share the interests and concerns of God that come to us in Christ and the Spirit. Friends are of one heart, and that is how charity has made us before God. To be of one heart and soul with God is to be a friend of God, to love what God loves, to cherish what God values, to want nothing more than whatever God wills. The purpose of the moral life, Thomas hints, is for us to become for God who God has always been for us, a friend who seeks our good and who wishes our perfect happiness, a friend who has our interests and well-being at heart; this is the possibility charity offers. When we can behold God as God has always beheld us, as another self, a friend whose happiness is perfectly our own, then beatitude has been gained. A lifetime of charity has made us enough like God to have union with God.[7]

However, we have to be careful about how we understand this idea of becoming "another self" to God. To speak this way does not mean we become God, nor does it mean there is no longer any difference between God and ourselves. Love brings likeness, not identity. In making us another self to God, charity does not abolish differences between God and ourselves; rather, it works for the union of hearts that is every friendship's perfection. The most perfect and lasting union requires a likeness based on goodness and love. If our perfect happiness consists in our perfect union with God, then this is nothing other than the relationship we have with God when we are another self to God. It does not mean we are lost in God or that God's love overwhelms our own; nor does it mean we are annihilated in God, as if God's love destroys our self. No, God's love does not destroy our self, it brings our self to its ultimate perfection, a self so imbued with God's goodness that we can consider ourselves not God, but another self to God.

There would be a problem in this idea of becoming another self to God if it meant there were no longer any differences between God and ourselves, but that is not so. Charity makes us like God, it does not make us God; indeed, if charity is truly friendship, it makes us more fully someone who is not God, it makes us more fully ourselves. If to become another self to God meant we became identical to God, then there could be no friendship with God. Friendships exist only where people are other. We can only have a friendship with someone who is not ourself. If charity made us identical to God, then our friendship with God would be over for we would no longer be the "other" every friendship requires. To say that in charity we become another self to God means the more we become like God, the more we become someone other than God, namely ourselves. In becoming godly, we become someone God is not, we become ourselves. By becoming another self to God we become someone most distinctively other than God, and it is exactly this perfection of otherness, an otherness rooted in the divine goodness, which enables the most splendid flourishing of friendship with God. We can only have a relationship of friendship when the friend remains other. What friendship achieves is not an identity of selves, but the most genuine differentiation fostered by a love for the most genuine good. The best kind of friendship makes for the best kind of self, and that is why the likeness to God charity brings is really the most radical individuation. We can consider God another self because in charity God's good is our good; however, it is in making God's good our own that we most fully become not God, but ourselves.

What happens in any friendship is that in some ways the friends become more alike, but in other ways they become increasingly differ-ent. As friendships grow, likeness increases inasmuch as the interests, concerns, values and ideals of the friends become similar. On the other hand, differences increase too, because the deeper and longer our friendships with others, the more we become ourselves. The same is true in our friendship with God. We become more like God because we learn to love what God loves, but we also become more unlike God because we become more genuinely ourselves. From loving God we grow into ourselves, that is what charity teaches us. To the degree we become like God in goodness we become someone other than God, the unique, splendid person God's love has always wanted us to be.

Finally, although to speak of God as another self does not mean God's self becomes our own, it does mean we cannot be ourself without God. When we tell a friend she is another self to us, we imply it is hard for us to imagine ourself without her. She is so integral to our life that to lose her friendship would be to lose a part of ourself. Friends are that important to us. They are substantial, irreplaceable parts of our lives, which is why to change our friends is to change ourselves. If this is true in every good friendship, it is also true in our friendship with God. To call God another self is a confession of need, a heartfelt acknowledgement that we need God in order to be. To speak of God as another self does not say charity makes us identical to God, but it does acknowledge that we have a self insofar as we share the life of God. To speak of God as another self is a reminder that what it means for us to be a self is to be God's friend, a reminder that God is the one by whom we always are. God is another self to us because our self is our friend-ship with God. What it means for any of us to be is to be God's friend, and that is why our fullest self is acquired when we are able to look upon God as another self.[8]

In this chapter we have explored what Thomas takes to be the grandest and most blessed possibility of our lives. It is charity, it is friendship with God. Thomas knows God loves us and we are called to love God, but he understands this love in a remarkably special way. It is the distinctive love of friendship, a love that promises an intimacy and union with God which bestows the happiness for which our hearts have always longed. Friendship is not any kind of relationship, and it is certainly more than mere fondness or affection. If someone is our friend we wish them well, but they wish us well, too—the benevolence is shared. A friendship is this mutual, ongoing delighting in shared goods, and the longer this is sustained the more each friend becomes for the other another self. Thomas sees all this happening in our love life with God. To be God's friend is to wish what is best for God and to seek it, as God has always done for us. It is to delight with God in what is best and most beautiful, and through that exchange to be transfigured in the goodness of God. The more that transfiguration occurs can we share the happiness God has always wanted for us because we have become enough like God in goodness to know God's joy. This is what is so special about charity's love. It puts no limit on the happiness God wants us to enjoy, and that is why it alone is the love that can bring peace to our hearts.

It is clear that in Aquinas's vision of the moral life everything turns on what we love. It is an ethic of the heart, an ethic of refined and noble affections. If we are to be reunited with God, we must learn to love well in every dimension of our lives. That is the work of the virtues, but for Aquinas, not surprisingly, the virtues take root in the passions, and that is the subject of chapter 5.

5. The Passions and Affections in the Moral Life: Exploring the Primacy of Love

For Aquinas the most important concern of the moral life is the development of our feelings according to what is best for us. We are naturally lovers, but we have to learn to love the right things in the right way. We must tutor our affections so that we respond rightly to all that stands before us, loving what is good, detesting what is evil, experiencing sorrow when something genuinely good is lost, anger when it is threatened, and fear when there is a chance it may be overcome. Contrary to what many think, and contrary to how Aquinas has so often been interpreted, what matters in the moral life is not denying the passions or trying to repress them, but cultivating them to empower us in doing good. The Christian moral life, Aquinas insisted, does not demand extirpating the passions, but transforming them. Morality needs the passions because it is only when there is something for which we care that we do anything at all. Thomas wants the feelings, the passions, and the emotions—he wants them all—but he wants them in the right way. For him, morality balances on cultivating the right kind of love, and letting that love direct our lives.

We know this already. The stronger we feel about something the easier it is for us to do it. If we love something deeply and passionately, we will devote ourselves to seeking it. We sense the danger of apathy. To be apathetic is to be unmoved by anything, to feel nothing; more poignantly, it is to be dead to all good. To love is to be alive to good, it is to experience the world's loveliness and to respond to it. When we love something we seek it, we set up our lives to attain it, and when we have gained what we love we find joy. This is Thomas's schema of the moral life, love at work seeking its completion in joy. Thomas knows we have to feel in order to act; that is why our passions and affections are so crucial to him. He does not dismiss them in his discussion of the moral life. For Aquinas, the passions and affections are the linchpin of

79

moral living because ultimately what becomes of us turns on what we love and how we love, on what we choose to make us happy and what will make us sad. Love informs all we do. Whatever we love we desire, and if we desire it we seek it through action. Our lives are a multitude of loves at work, each of those loves guiding, shaping, and transforming our lives. Thomas knows this. He cannot have a moral theology fit for men and women unless he takes seriously the role of the passions and affections in our lives. Because our feelings are such an elementary, indispensable fact of our existence, Thomas must speak to them, he must find their role in the moral life, he must learn what they mean, how they function, and why we have been endowed with them. To dismiss them is to ignore a vital part of us, to call them irrelevant in discussions of morality is to fashion an ethic that can only do harm.

Feeling is at the heart of life. Could it also be the heart of goodness? This is what Thomas wonders when he begins his analysis of the passions and affections. He knows there must be a way for our emotions to facilitate, not hinder, our quest for goodness. His hunch is that in order to be good we have to be committed to something, there has to be something we care about, some basic passion driving our lives. He knows good people are great lovers, and if this is so he has to figure out what good people love. He knows this much: moral wholeness lies not in circumventing the passions, but in cultivating them through the right kind of love. We need a love that will make us both happy and good. It is this Thomas has in mind when he begins his exploration of our hearts. We shall consider all this now by looking first at what the passions indicate about our human nature and how it is completed, and secondly by looking specifically at the passion of love and why it has primacy for Aquinas. Our reflections in this chapter will be tied to Thomas's analysis of the passions and emotions in questions twenty-two and twenty-six of the Prima Secundae (*ST,* I-II, 22, 2; 26, 2).

I.   TO BE HUMAN IS TO BE PASSIONATE: WE ARE MADE TO RECEIVE THE WORLD

The most general term Aquinas uses to explain the passions and affections is "appetite." It is a fitting description. We know what it means to have an appetite. It is to hunger for something we lack. If we have not eaten for a long time we have an appetite for food. If we are lonely and sad we have an appetite for companions or activity. If we feel harried, we may have an appetite for solitude. If we are worn down by work and daily responsibilities, we have an appetite for leisure. An appetite is a tendency toward something we perceive as good, but lack. We want it because we think it will be good for us, but because we lack it we experience need. We are needy for the food that will end our hunger, needy for the friends who can console us, needy for the silence that can quiet our lives. To have an appetite is to turn toward and seek whatever we think is good and necessary for ourselves.

Appetites begin in a recognition of need. We sense our incompletion and we see before us something we think will ease it, that is why it strikes us as good. We want something because it appears to be at least a partial answer to our neediness. Recognizing its goodness, we respond by reaching out to it, by seeking and trying to possess it. We have appetites because we experience so deeply our incompleteness. We live alertly for whatever might be an answer to our neediness, and when we find something we feel will bring us closer to fullness, we desire it. Appetites are rooted in need; they are nature's way of dealing with our incompletion. An appetite is rooted in the awareness that there is something we lack but need to possess if we are to grow and develop. But they are also rooted in the awareness that these are goods we cannot give ourselves. They stand outside us and apart from us. They lure us, beckon to us, and entice us by their value. These are goods we cannot give, but only receive, so in experiencing their goodness we reach out to them in order to make them part of our lives.

Human Beings Are Creatures of Appetites

There is in Aquinas's description of appetites a picture of what it means to be human. A human being is a creature of appetites, of powerful, perduring tendencies. A human being is one whose very nature is appetite, whose whole being is a turning toward all those goods which promise fullness of life. We are hungry for completion, famished for a wholeness we can only receive. We are alive with a sense of our neediness. We know the hunger for friendship, we have been starved for love and affection. We thirst for knowledge and insight, for beauty and wisdom. We are touched by the loveliness of a beautiful day, but even more so by the kindness of a stranger. We feel incompleteness in our bones. It is the root of our being, so we naturally respond in interest and hope to all the goods of our world that can fill what is lacking in our lives. We are appetites, we are needy creatures hungering to possess the goods that will complete us, which may, incidentally, help us understand why bread and wine are such fitting symbols by which a hungry people celebrates eucharist.[1]

It is important to appreciate that the passions and affections, as appetites, are active only in a secondary sense. True, an appetite suggests that we reach out toward something we experience as good, but the activity does not begin with us, but in the object to which we are attracted. Appetites signal activity, they describe how we move toward what is good, but their activity is a response to something whose goodness has already acted upon us. Appetites respond, they reach out only because they have first felt the touch of another thing's goodness. Consider how we know something to be good. We do not declare its value, we feel its value. Hearing a Mozart symphony, it is not so much we who say it is beautiful, but the music which says so to us. Standing before the Grand Canyon, it is not we who bestow its value, but the canyon which says, "I am beautiful" to us. We react to a Mozart symphony, to the Grand Canyon, to a painting by Monet because each first speaks its goodness to us. We respond to a goodness apprehended, to a value deeply perceived. Or what is it like to fall in love with another person? The very language we use to describe such experiences signals that we seek to know someone only because we have first suffered their unmistakable goodness. We are attracted to them because their preciousness has somehow moved straight to our soul. That is why so often we are in love with people before we are consciously aware of it. Something about them, their goodness, their beauty, their singularity, has spoken to us, affected us, touched us so deeply that we ineluctably move out to them in response. If we desire anything, it is only because we have first experienced its goodness. Having known its goodness, we move toward it in order to know it more fully, in order not to lose the goodness we have found. This is how Thomas explains the process:

> Correspondingly, the effect produced in the appetite by a desirable object is a sense of affinity with it, a feeling of its attractiveness; then this gives rise to a movement of the appetite towards the object. For there is a certain circularity in the appetitive process, as Aristotle remarks; first the object works on the appetite, imprinting itself there, as one might say; then the appetite moves towards the object, with the purpose of actually possessing it; so the process ends where it began (*ST,* I-II, 26,2).

An Anatomy of Love

What is happening here? What is Thomas explaining? He offers an anatomy of love, and says love commences not so much with ourselves, but with what is loved—Thomas calls it the desirable object—acting on us in such a way that it changes us. This is what Thomas means when he says "the effect produced in the appetite by a desirable object is a sense of affinity with it, a feeling of its attractiveness." The desirable object works on us, its goodness breaks through and begins to change us. We feel its goodness, it touches us; however briefly, it becomes part of who we are. Put differently, we act toward what we love because it has first acted on us. We are not initially active. At first we are passive inasmuch as we do not create these values, we suffer them, we experience them, we are moved and intrigued by them. We are passive inasmuch as we act only because we are first acted upon. We suffer the world's goodness—we feel its touch—and then we reach out in love. We respond to a world rich in value, a world enticing, complex, and abundant in wonders. We feel its goodness and are moved by it. The goodness of what stands before us is impressed on us. That is why we are enchanted with a beautiful painting or a lovely flower, and it is also why we fall in love with a beautiful person. The goodness of life thrusts itself through and leaves its mark on our souls. To be marked by another thing's loveliness is to be changed forever. We cannot leave this goodness behind, it is part of who we are. We cannot forget it because it endures in our hearts. This is the "effect" Thomas speaks of when he explains how something good changes us, imbuing us with a sense of affinity or attraction to it. We feel a kinship with all things of loveliness because something of the goodness of each has entered us. We seek these things because elements of their preciousness have become part of the fabric of our lives. We are inclined to them because something of their goodness has already slipped inside our souls.

Why is it there are certain people we never get over? Or why is it there are people we have not seen for years who still live so powerfully in our hearts? Some people enter our lives so compellingly that we are never quite the same. Even in their absence we feel their presence. Even if we know we shall never see them again, we cannot act as if they had never been part of our lives. They have left their mark. They have irremediably changed us. For better or worse, we cannot act as if they had never been known. They are part of our history, they are inseparable from our identity. For us to be ourself is to know ourself as somehow marked by them. Why is this so? How come certain people affect us so lastingly? This is what Aquinas means when he says "first the object works on the appetite, imprinting itself there. . . ." Something of these people is left within us, is imprinted there and continues to shape us. That is why they can so suddenly come to mind, why after years of absence we can feel their presence so forcefully. Other people do "work on us." There is something about them that forever is imprinted on our hearts. They enter our lives and leave something of themself behind. Something of their goodness passes over to us.

But if it marks us it also changes us. The effect of another person's goodness is not cosmetic, it is heartfelt. Thomas puts this rather arcanely when he explains, "The term 'passion' denotes the effect produced in a thing when it is acted upon by some agent" (*ST,* I-II, 26,2), but the import of what he says is not esoteric at all. Thomas is talking about how other people and other things change us, work on us, reshape us. He is grappling to express how deeply and enduringly we are influenced by our world, and what he wants to show is that none of these influences is peripheral. They are personal and they are lasting, which is why we have passion for them, and why, having suffered their goodness, we reach out in response. The change of which Thomas speaks is an interior transformation of ourselves. We are modified inwardly by receiving another person's preciousness, and having felt it as part of our soul, we seek it as a further definition of ourselves. Because we have taken on another person's goodness, they are integral to our identity. We reach out to them because we cannot imagine ourselves without them. This is why Thomas says "the first effect" produced in us by the object "is love, which is simply a feeling of the object's attractiveness" (*ST,* I-II, 26,2). We love them because we have suffered their goodness, because something of their undeniable value has broken through to us, not inertly or fleetingly, but so completely that they have produced in us an inclination toward themselves and a sense of affinity with them. We love them now, not only because we have felt their goodness, but also because they have become part of ourselves; we seek them because we sense they are where we belong.

Love: An Abiding Openness to All That Is Good

We are made to receive something. This is the heart of Aquinas's anthropology. We are not closed-off, self-sufficient individuals, but creatures of such poignant need that we are fashioned to be open, shaped to embrace all the goods that bless us with fuller life. We are made to be receptive, and such abiding openness to the goodness of others and life is the most basic and natural fact about us. We misunderstand ourselves if we lack this hospitality to life. We do irreparable harm to ourselves if we are guarded and closed. And we die if we never receive anyone at all. We are made to receive something; that is why we flourish when we love and die when we hate, why reconciliation and healing are so indispensable, and why hardened, brittle, unforgiving hearts are awful. We are made to take on life, other people and, surely, God. We are made to be filled with the life our world offers, and ultimately to be filled with the vitality of God. And it is not only true of us, it is true for our universe. Love is the universal fact, expression of a universal longing. Love begins as allurement, and it is precisely this allurement that holds the cosmos together.[2] We are made to be lovers, all of us, and we are at our best when we are this universe of love, each one giving and receiving, everyone blessing and being blessed. This is how Aquinas sees us, creatures of longing needing to be loved, each becoming a source of life and a center of rescue for the other.

Such is Aquinas's vision of our moral universe. It is a universe of deep interrelationship, a universe of abiding mutual influence as each thing acts on everything else, producing a symmetry of neediness and giftedness, of lack and the means to make whole. We are connected in our need, but also in our ability to bless and enrich. We share an openness for what we cannot offer ourselves, but we can offer to another what we can only receive. This is the beauty of Thomas's moral universe—each one blessing another with the life she or he must also receive. When Thomas says so succinctly that "the term 'passion' denotes the effect produced in a thing when it is acted upon by some agent," what he denotes is a universe in which everything is passionate because everything has received, a cosmos in which everything hungers, because everything has known something else's goodness. It is a picture of all of us being touched, acted upon, and influenced by the multitude of "agents" in our world, whether that be another person, beautiful scenery, the power of a poem, or the magic of a wonderful meal.

To be influenced by all these things is to take away with us whatever makes them good. Thomas says we receive their "form" (*ST*, I-II, 26,2). The "form" is whatever is most distinctive and unique about another thing, it is what identifies it as one thing instead of another. To receive the form of something means that what is most personal about it is now part of ourselves. It means we are no longer totally distinct because something of another lives within us. Is not this what happens when we love another person? We are no longer totally other because we have taken on something of the person we love. They really do live within us, they become part of our soul. This is why we love them all the more, why the longer we love them the more we desire them, and why no intimacy with them ever seems enough. They are too much part of us to be forgotten, and so much part of us that we can never embrace them enough. Having suffered their goodness, our lives are intermingled, our souls striving to become one.

This is what Thomas means when he speaks of the passions and affections, and what he has in mind when he sees us as creatures of appetite. He is struggling to express why we love at all and what happens to us when we do love. He wants to understand as best he can why we so fervently seek what we have found to be good. First, he says, it is because we have experienced its goodness in the deepest possible way. Its goodness has become part of us—we have acquired something of its form—and because of this we feel a sense of affinity or kinship with it. What we love is no longer something wholly other, no longer anything alien or strange. It is personal, it is part of who we are, it is inseparable from our understanding of ourselves. Secondly, he says that because we have received its goodness, we begin to move towards it in love. In the first phase we are passive, we do not act, we receive; however, in the second phase we are active, responsive, intentional, we reach out in love to what we know is good. In this second sense the passions are appetites that relate us to what we have come to love in the hope that we might possess it. This is why Thomas says the whole process ends where it began. Because something lovely has spoken to us, we desire it, and because we desire it we act in order to make it part of our lives. And so the moral life consists in this: the effect of something good and lovely upon us, and our response to its goodness in action. Something acts on us, we act in response. This is Aquinas's sense of the moral life. It is being touched and reaching out, being acted upon and moving toward. Consciously or not, we move through life with open hearts. What matters most is learning how open hearts are to be filled.

II. WHAT IT MEANS TO CALL
LOVE A PASSION

Aquinas's moral theology argues elegantly that we are not yet who we should be, and that we do not have within us what is lacking for our completion. What is requisite for wholeness stands outside us.

Our restoration is not something we can provide ourselves, it is only something we can receive; thus, it is not so much a question of self-development, but of being developed by another. For Aquinas, our incompletion does not signify that we merely need more time to perfect ourselves; rather, being incomplete signals we lack within ourselves the resources for our completion. We are not only deficient, we are inherently deficient. What we lack for wholeness we are compelled to receive: our completion will be a gift.

This is why Thomas calls love a passion. A passion is a sign of deficiency, a confession of need. The word passion signifies the need for further development, it speaks of incompleteness yearning for growth; however, it also recognizes that wholeness is not something we can bestow on ourselves, but is something we acquire through the agency of another. To say that love is the key to our moral deliverance, and to identify it as a passion, is to know that our perfection comes by receiving a good we not only lack, but by nature are incapable of giving ourselves. As human beings we stand in absolute need: we come to wholeness only by suffering a good other than our own. As Aquinas explains, "Now passion or passivity implies, by its very nature, some sort of deficiency: a thing is passive in so far as it is in potentiality to being actualized and thus improved" (*ST,* I-II, 22,2).

In this passage Thomas argues that the deficiency we suffer as human beings is remedied not by ourselves, but by someone who can offer us what we cannot offer ourselves. Passion not only registers need, it also registers receptivity, for it suggests that whatever wholeness is lacking is brought to us through the agency of someone else. We are restored by someone other working on us, we are healed through an agency other than our own. By using the language of "potentiality," Thomas admits our indigence can be overcome, but he immediately adds that this occurs not primarily through our own efforts, but through our openness to whatever has the goodness and power to draw us more fully to life. If "a thing is passive in so far as it is in potentiality to being actualized and thus improved," it is clear for Aquinas that our utmost improvement is not a question of our own efforts, but of how much we are willing to suffer the love of one who can make us whole. We do stand "in a relation of potentiality to actuality," but what Thomas insists is that the distance between who we are now and who we are called to be is the work of one whose love provides for us what we could never provide ourselves. To speak of love as a passion not only means something more must happen to us, but also that this something more is not a question of our own efforts, but of another love working within us. We stand "in a relation of potentiality to actuality," a relation of promise to possible fulfillment. But what Aquinas intimates is that our fulfillment comes not at our own hands, but through the caress of a better love. As we shall see, it is precisely this insight that stands behind Aquinas's conviction that the virtues are brought to perfection not by our own efforts, but through the Spirit of Love working within us.

Why Love Is the Utmost Vulnerability

This changes how we think of love. We can still speak of love as perfecting, but must do so in a different sense. It is perfecting because its express activity is to hand us over to whatever completes us. There is a strategy to love, and it is to open us increasingly to the Love by whom all things are. If we are brought to life by God and others, then our love perfects not because it develops some innate capacity within us, but because it further avails us to those who can make us whole. Love is the openness we need to live. It is precisely the vulnerability that does not destroy us, but brings us more fully to life, because it is in love that we stand in relationship to all that can heal and restore. To be human is to receive what we lack for wholeness, it is to be vulnerable to whatever can bring us most fully to life. The more open we are to such goodness, the more lastingly our neediness is overcome. It is openness to the best and most perfecting that heals us, and so it is with God in mind that Aquinas writes the following:

> An excellence obviously increases as the first and unique source of the excellence is approached—somewhat as the brightness of a lighted object increases as it approaches the source of light. A deficiency increases, however, not with proximity to, but with distance from what is perfect and supreme: that is precisely what makes a thing defective. Naturally then, the less a thing departs from the appropriate source, the less defective it is. So it is that defects are commonly slight to begin with, and grow worse as time goes by (*ST,* I-II, 22,2).

This is probably the most pithy summary of Aquinas's moral theology: the nearer we are to God, the better we are, because God is the excellence by which all things are made good. It is not we, strictly speaking, who make ourselves good, but we who are transformed, renewed, and restored by the love of God acting within us, healing us, redeeming us. This is why calling love a passion and making it the soil and root of the virtues may be Aquinas's most brilliant methodological move; it is certainly the heart of his moral theology. A passion means something is perfected the more it receives from the source of its perfection. It cannot perfect itself because the source of its perfection lies outside itself. Aquinas hints this when he writes, "The term passion implies . . . that the patient is drawn to something in the agent" (*ST,* I-II, 22,2). What we are drawn to in the agent who is God is the goodness and life we need to be saved, a goodness we can receive, but never equal.

But notice, too, the image Thomas uses in this passage. In the moral life we are "patients" and God is the "agent," which means God is the one who acts, we are the ones who must be open to receive. We are patients being treated and healed by God's love. It means we stand in need of a healing we can only receive, and it is from God that we receive it. It means we are broken, wounded, often shattered in our lives, and are restored not through our own determination, but through our suppleness to God. God is the Good Samaritan who rescues us on our journey, the One who stops to carry us along. In the moral life, we are the patients and God is the healer, the One who watches out for us, caresses us, binds up our wounds and brings us to life. It means the moral life is essentially a healing of incompleteness through the only Love that can make all things whole. For Thomas, the moral life is to "suffer" or "undergo" God, to allow ourselves to be acted upon by the love that heals and restores. The moral life is an ongoing rehabilitation in which lives sometimes wrecked by confusion or ravaged by hurts are cleansed and restored through the love we can never rival, but always receive. It is God acting upon us in the Spirit that accounts for our restoration; thus, the closer we draw to God through love, the more intense and perfecting is God's saving love upon us, the more inescapable is that love, and the more penetrating its effects. For Aquinas, the moral life is the never-ending rehabilitation of ourselves through the blessed love that redeems. That we shall never be good enough to merit this love does not matter; we need only be humble enough to receive it.

Charity Is Passionate Openness for God

What might designating love a passion do to our understanding of charity? If love as a passion is essentially receptivity, then charity is impassioned receptivity for God. This alters our understanding of charity as a virtue. To speak of charity as passionate openness for God does not mean it is no virtue, but it may not be the virtue we customarily think. If love is a passion and charity is passion for God, then as a virtue its express function is to open us further to God. If a passion is the capacity to be actualized by something else, charity is the virtue that works to leave us supple before God. Charity is an activity, but as a virtue charity's activity is essentially openness. We hinted this in chapter 4 when we spoke of what it means to have friendship with God. Charity is the virtue of friendship with God, but we saw that such friendship is only possible when we become enough like God in goodness to be "another self" to God. If this is to happen, we must practice an extraordinary receptivity to God. In other words, if charity works toward friendship with God, it begins in passion for God, for it is only through an abiding willingness to "suffer" God completely that we gain the likeness necessary to speak of God as friend. By rooting charity in this passionate longing for God, Aquinas demonstrates that charity must change us before it can complete us.

We can already guess how this analysis of the passion of love will give Aquinas a very different understanding of the virtues. Yes, he has an ethic of virtue, but they are clearly virtues of a different kind. There is a paradox woven through Aquinas's account of the virtues, but it is a paradox that can be glimpsed only when the connection between the passions and the virtues is acknowledged. The mistake in so many studies of Aquinas's moral theology was failing to spot the link between his study of the passions and affections, and his theory of the virtues. We cannot understand rightly what Aquinas takes a virtue to be, unless we see it in light of the love from which it emerges. To understand what Aquinas means by the virtues—especially those born from charity's love—we cannot consider them apart from the passions and affections because it is the passion of love that gives the virtues shape and meaning. For Aquinas, the virtues are principally strategies of love. The virtues are works of love because each virtue expresses in a particular way our primary love at work. Thomas never considers the virtues in themselves, but always in relation to the passions from which they emerge and according to which they take their meaning. Because the virtues are anchored in love, and love is a passion, the more we grow in the virtues the more we realize how totally dependent we are on another's love.

The paradox in Aquinas's understanding of the virtues is that through the activity of virtues born from charity, we grow not more independent or self-sufficient, but more reliant upon God. To grow in charity's virtues is to grow in divine dependence, to allow ourselves increasingly to be acted upon by God. The paradox is this: the more active we are in charity's love, the more active God can be toward us.

The paradox is that the stronger we are in charity's virtues, the more defenseless we grow before God. There is surely a twist to how Thomas understands the virtues, but it is a twist we can see only when we acknowledge the connection between the virtues and the love which forms them. The more charity grows in us, the harder God is to resist, because if we grow in such passionate love for God we cannot help but suffer God's love more completely. To increase charity is to grow weaker in the ways we can resist God, stronger in the ways we can receive God.

This is madness to anyone schooled to think the virtues are those activities by which we perfect ourselves, but it is an understanding of the virtues that cannot be avoided once we consider their connection to love and know what it means to call love a passion. This does not mean the virtues don't perfect us, they just don't perfect us as we usually think. They perfect us because when we love we let ourselves be changed, because when we suffer or undergo the love of God we are healed, because the more we act toward God in the virtues the more we receive the love that redeems. As articulating a passion for God, any virtue formed in charity is a way we are changed by the love that makes us God's friend.

Why Charity Makes Us Godly

And that change is startling. To suffer something is to receive something, it is to take on something we did not have before. This is how Aquinas says we grow in the goodness of God. What happens when we seek to love God as friend is that through the passionate openness of charity we absorb the loveliness of God. This is why we become what we love. Since love is a passion, when we love we are formed according to our beloved. Love always changes us, but it changes us in virtue of the loved one. To love is to make ourselves vulnerable to what is not ourselves. Love is the most drastic vulnerability because it not only opens us to the other, but opens us to them in such a way that we allow ourselves to suffer the very thing that makes them other than ourselves, and with God this is the goodness of God. In love we are defined not through ourselves, but through what we love. To love is to be determined by the loved one, to receive them fully into our being. Love is a handing over, a surrendering of ourselves to the goodness of the one we love. To love is to be remade according to that goodness. There is a conversion at work here, a transfiguration, but it is utterly beyond us inasmuch as the change is governed by the one we love. What happens then in charity when we love with passionate openness to God, is that we are remade according to the goodness of God. Charity is conversion because to love God is to lose one kind of self and acquire another, a self that is shaped in God's goodness.

And so there is something beautiful, but also something unnerving to charity. To love God in charity means we lose control over our life precisely where the risk is greatest: we lose control over our self. To have charity is to be recentered on God, not only because God becomes our primary attachment, but more significantly because God becomes the One by whom we are. To love God in charity is to give God the unnerving control of being able to influence us. We said earlier that we can never escape the influence of what we love, and this is why. To love is to let the other have us, but in the quite strong sense of being the one by whom we are made known. To love God in charity is to be made by God, it is to entrust ourselves to the power of a goodness we cannot control.

All this suggests if we are ever to love we have to let ourselves die. Love requires dying, at least dying to excessive self-control, dying to unhealthy self-attachment. To love, large parts of ourselves have to die. We have to die in the sense that we let go of our life. We have to die in the sense that we finally surrender to someone else's goodness. We have to die if we are to love, because to love is to be possessed by someone else's goodness, and with charity it is to be possessed by the goodness of God. To love, as the gospel puts it, we must suffer the loss of one kind of self and trust in the self formed by the goodness of God.

We have traveled far in this chapter. We discussed the role of the passions and affections in the moral life. We noted how important our feelings are for Aquinas and how he sees them empowering our growth in goodness. We spoke of ourselves as creatures of appetite hungering for all the goods we lack and need to be whole. And we noted that love opens us to be shaped, changed, blessed, and enriched by all those goods acting upon us. This may be another person, a work of art or a scene from nature, but it is also God. The strategy of Aquinas's moral theology is to render us supple to the gracious influence of God, for it is when we suffer the love and goodness and mercy of God that we are healed and made whole.

But this is not easy. We may have a deep desire for God in our lives, and we may want friendship and union with God more than anything else, but there is much to dissuade us. The moral life begins in love and moves to joy, but is often interrupted by adversity. The ebb and flow of daily life wears us down. Like Stephen Dedalus in James Joyce's *A Portrait of the Artist as a Young Man,* we "grow weary of ardent ways." Sometimes tragedy intervenes and disrupts, occasionally misfortune is so discouraging that our desire to be good dims to a glimmer. At other times we simply tire of routine and the press of responsibilities, and hunger not for goodness but for escape. All this is part of our moral experience and Thomas must address it. To see how he does, we must probe more deeply his analysis of the emotions and the different functions they have in his schema of the moral life. We shall consider this in chapter 6.

6. The Passions and Affections in the Moral Life: Finding the Strength to Go On

I met a woman on a retreat once who had become too familiar with adversity. When she came to talk to me she was so troubled she could not speak. She handed me a piece of paper that was a map of her soul. On it she had jotted: "depression," "loneliness," "rejection," "anger," "despair." It was her despair that worried me, her anger that gave me hope. As long as she felt angry, she cared enough for her life to want to change it. But if her anger were extinguished by despair she was in trouble, for then she would no longer believe anything good was possible; she would see no reason to act.

Life is a matter of going on. One of the dominant images for the moral life we have used in this book is motion. We spoke of men and women as acting for the sake of an end. We described our moral behavior as intentional, and noted that all intentional behavior is a matter of moving from what we want to have to possessing it. Happiness implied movement, too, because we discovered we were happy when we were one with what we loved. When we began to study the passions and affections, this image of motion continued. If our passions indicate our need, then the moral life is a matter of overcoming deficiency by moving closer to what will perfect us. Action, growth, development, movement—they are all images of the moral life. As Aquinas saw it, the moral life is the saga of moving toward what we love so that we might find joy.

But joy is never easily attained because much imperils possessing it. We confront obstacles and our enthusiasm lags. Adversity makes us wonder if happiness is beyond our reach. Fate and misfortune jeopardize our growth in the good, sometimes robbing us of hope. Thomas took all this seriously. What concerned him is that too much bad luck might leave us so dispirited that we would forsake the moral life altogether, giving up before we had reached the end.

We need some way to deal with adversity in the moral life. To address this problem, Thomas turned to the passions and emotions, for he saw them empowering us to go on when we were tempted to despair. In this chapter we shall discuss how Thomas distinguished the emotions and what he understood their function in the moral life to be. Our analysis will stem from Thomas's own treatment of these themes in question 23 of the Prima Secundae where he deals with the classification of the emotions, and question 25 in which he shows how all of them are related.

I. THE TWO GROUPS OF EMOTIONS AND WHAT THEY MEAN

Thomas divides the emotions into two groups. The first he calls the "concupiscible" or "affective" emotions, the second the "irascible" or "spirited" emotions. The affective emotions represent a relationship we have to something insofar as it is either good or evil. There are six affective emotions that capture this relationship: love, hatred, desire, aversion, joy, sadness. If we are attracted to something because it seems good to us, the emotion we experience is love. Love is the first and primary affective emotion. If we love something we move toward it in the hope of making it our own, and so the second emotion we experience is desire. If through desire we come to possess what we love, then the emotion we feel is joy.

On the other hand, if something strikes us as evil or harmful, we do not love it, we hate or despise it, and since we despise it we do not move toward it in desire, but away from it in aversion. And if we cannot escape what we abhor, we experience not joy but sorrow.

We see, then, that there are six affective emotions, each registering a response to something as either good or evil. What emotion we experience depends on whether what is before us is lovely or horrible, and how we might stand in relation to it. If it is good, we love it and thus desire it. If it is horrible, we despise it and move away in aversion. If we touch what we love we find joy, but if we are touched by what we abhor—if we cannot escape the evil—we experience sorrow. These are the six affective emotions, and they can be divided into three pairs. Love is matched with its opposite, hatred, desire with aversion, and joy with sorrow or sadness. This is how Thomas describes the basic affective movement of our lives:

> Now the good as good can never be the object of an impulse away from itself, but only of one towards itself: nothing shuns the good as good: it is precisely what all things want. Similarly, nothing wants an evil as evil: it is precisely what things shun; therefore an evil as such is never the object of an impulse towards itself, but only of one away from itself. Hence each of the affective emotions whose object is a good is a movement towards that good, viz. love, desire, and pleasure; and each of them whose object is an evil is a movement away from it, viz. hatred, aversion or disgust, and sadness (*ST,* I-II, 23, 2).

We can see in this description of the six affective emotions an overview of the moral life. Each pair corresponds to one of the three phases of our moral experience. The moral life commences in love, works through desire, and is completed in joy. Love is first because we begin to act only when we have been attracted to something good and feel an affinity for it; however, hatred is our reaction to something we have come to know is bad, especially if it threatens our good. Secondly, there is desire. Desire is the emotion by which we move toward what we love, but aversion is what we feel for what is evil. Finally, when we possess what we love and our desire is satisfied, the emotion we experience is joy; but sadness comes upon us when instead of being united to our good we are brought to evil. Love, desire, union, that is the plot of the moral life, and this is how Thomas describes it:

> When the movement in question is that of an appetitive faculty, it is a good which plays the part of the attracting agent, and an evil the part of the repelling one. First then, the good produces in the faculty an inclination towards it, a sense of affinity with it, a sense that the good and itself are naturally fitted for each other; this is the emotion called love. The corresponding contrary, when it is some evil to the agent, is hatred. Second, if the good is not yet possessed, it sets up in the faculty a motion towards attaining this good which it has come to love. This is desire; the opposite is aversion or disgust. Third, once the good is possessed, the faculty finds repose in its possession. This is pleasure or joy; the opposite is sadness or grief (*ST,* I-II, 23,4).

We can see our own moral odyssey reflected in Aquinas's account of the affective emotions. We move toward what we love, but away from what we fear or despise. We hate what threatens our good, so we strive to avoid it. If we arrive at our good we are joyous, but if evil prevails we are sad. The plot of the moral life is given through the affective emotions, for each represents our standing to what we love. We can picture it this way:

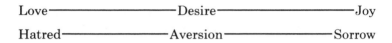

Love————————————Desire————————————Joy
Hatred————————————Aversion————————————Sorrow

Learning to Love What Is Good and Abhor What Is Evil

This sketch of the moral life reminds us how important the proper formation of our sentiments is for moral development. For Aquinas, moral wholeness requires that we learn to love what is genuinely good and hate what is truly evil, and to do both with passion and zeal. Virtuous people are fired with a zeal for what is genuinely good; likewise, they passionately abhor what is evil and false. Their virtue is not bland, but inspired. They do not do good out of duty or fear, but because they love the good. Similarly, they avoid evil because they despise it.

For Aquinas, authentic virtue stems from authentic love. We can be good only when we do good because we love what is good. We are not virtuous when we do good from fear or expectation; no, we are virtuous when we do good because we have cultivated a passion for it. Growth in goodness requires learning to love what is good and hate what is evil. There are some things that should attract us, but other things that should disgust us. If we are good, some things ought never be seen as possibilities for us; some behavior, some ways of life ought to remain unthinkable. Virtuous people do not entertain some options because they know they are evil and they abhor evil.

If becoming virtuous hinges on cultivating the right kind of affections, then goodness is a matter of strong feeling. We ought to have strong feelings in our lives, but if we are to become virtuous we need to feel strongly about what is good, but likewise to feel strongly against all that is evil. We need to be repulsed by certain possibilities and truly sad if they befall us. Some things must remain a scandal to us—options we would never consider—and some things should really frighten us: cruelty to others, abuse, exploitation, betrayal. Certain things should remain unthinkable to us, for if we begin to entertain them we gradually lose our abhorrence for them, and that is morally dangerous.

For instance, what is the danger in entertaining temptation? It is not benign because to flirt with temptation is to consider seriously something we should never come to desire. Even if we initially do so innocently, if we contemplate temptation long enough, the unthinkable eventually seems possible. By considering it, our feeling about it changes. It no longer seems distasteful. The point is, the longer we consider some things, the more quickly do we lose our abhorrence for them.

Aids to Our Moral Adventure: A Look At the Spirited Emotions

Seeing the moral life as movement toward what is good and away from what is evil sounds easy enough; in fact, it sounds too easy, and Thomas knew this. It would be easy if once we discovered our good we simply could act to possess it, but the moral life is seldom that smooth. There are things both within us and outside us that hinder our progress to the good. We need only consider why sometimes it is so difficult to be good. There is much within and without us that frustrates our love; there is so much working against us, whether that be our own weakness, our divided hearts, or the misfortune that can so powerfully undermine our belief that what we love can truly be had. The moral life is seldom purely progress in the good. Most often it is struggle, frequently it is disappointment, almost always it is hard. As the Greek epics and tragedies illustrate, the moral life is often a contest in which we try to make good on what we cherish, but suffer setbacks and discouragement; sometimes we are so dispirited we despair.

We can see this in our own lives. We begin with much enthusiasm, but eventually something occurs that challenges our zeal. We encounter adversity. We suffer unexpected misfortunes. We are visited by bad luck. We think our life is under control, but something breaks in and upends our confidence. It can be an illness, the loss of a job, the death of a relationship. Whatever it is, we feel the loss. We are discouraged, listless, and depressed. We begin to believe the good we seek is not possible for us. We feel defeated. We are edging to despair.

This is why Thomas says we need a second group of emotions, the "irascible" or "spirited" emotions. These emotions assist us when the good we seek is difficult to attain and evil hard to avoid. Sometimes what we love is under attack—or we feel under attack—and we need something extra to help us. There are periods of extreme hardship in our lives when we must find strength to continue. It is exactly at these moments that the spirited emotions come into play. As the word suggests, they are engaged when we are dispirited. Sometimes it is an occasion of extreme misfortune, or at other times we simply tire in our desire to be good. Thomas first speaks of them when he distinguishes the spirited emotions from the affective:

> In deciding therefore which passions and emotions belong to the spirited appetite and which to the affective, one must begin by recalling the respective objects of these two faculties. We found that the object of the affective faculty is sense-good and sense-evil, i.e., the pleasurable or the painful. But there are times when the soul finds that the acquisition of some good or the avoidance of some evil is possible only with difficulty, or even by fighting; it is beyond our ready power and control. So it is that the object of the spirited appetite is a sense-good or sense-evil as arduous, i.e., insofar as its acquisition or avoidance involves some kind of difficulty or struggle.
>
> The emotions of the affective appetite are therefore those which bear upon sense-good or sense-evil pure and simple: joy and sorrow, love and hatred, and the like. The emotions of the spirited appetite, on the other hand, are those which bear upon sense-good or sense-evil as arduous, i.e., insofar as it is difficult to attain or avoid: courage, fear, hope, and the like (*ST,* I-II, 23,1).

There are, then, five spirited emotions. They describe our relationship to our good when it is difficult to attain, or when something evil is hard to avoid. If there is something we want but it is not easily had, this arouses the emotion of hope; however, if the difficulty besetting us seems overwhelming, despair is what we feel. If the evil we want to avoid lurks near, we feel fear; however, because we have to face this evil, we need courage. The final spirited emotion is anger, and anger is aroused when what we love is under attack.

It is important to note, however, that the spirited emotions are secondary to the affective. They take their meaning from the affective emotions because they come into play only when adversity, misfortune, or discouragement threaten our quest for the good. If nothing challenges our love for the good, the spirited emotions are dormant. They exist for the sake of the affective emotions; that is, they stand at the service of our good and assist us in obtaining it when doing so is difficult. For example, when we are discouraged and tempted to give up, the spirited emotion of hope arises to empower us to continue. Or when it is difficult to pursue what we love because many things oppose us, there arises the spirited emotion of courage which enables us to stand fast and endure. Or when something we had hoped to avoid besets us and threatens our good, we feel the emotion of anger. Aquinas explains the status of the spirited emotions in the moral life, and how they stand in relation to the affective:

> If the object is a good not yet possessed, we have either hope or despair. If it is an evil which has not yet befallen one, we have either fear or courage. If it is a good already possessed, there will be no corresponding emotion in the spirited appetite; for it is no longer a good to be attained only with difficulty, as we have seen. But if it is an evil which is already in process of taking place, the emotion of anger is aroused.
>
> One sees then that there are three pairs of emotions belonging to the affective appetite: love and hatred, desire and aversion, pleasure and sadness. There are also three in the spirited appetite: hope and despair; fear and courage; and anger, which has no contrary. The emotions therefore comprise eleven distinct species, six in the affective appetite and five in the spirited (*ST,* I-II, 23,4).

As Aquinas's explanation indicates, we have the spirited emotions only because we first have the affective. It is precisely because we love something and want to possess it that we need hope, courage, and anger, precisely because there is something we desire that there are also things we fear and things which tempt us to despair. The spirited emotions take their meaning from the affective because if there were not love there would be no reason to hope or to have courage or to be angry. The spirited emotions cannot exist independently of the affective because their rationale is to safeguard what we love. Take away the object of our love, and you also take away the reason for hope and courage, as well as the reason for fear or despair. Without some love at the center of our lives, hope makes no sense for we do not know what to hope for and what we want to avoid that causes despair. Similarly, without love courage makes no sense either because we have no reason to endure. Without the affective emotions, particularly love, the spirited emotions have no point. Thomas captures this when he writes,

> The spirited emotions are therefore midway between those affective emotions which involve movement towards some good or away from some evil, and those which involve repose

in one or other of them. One sees then that the emotions of the spirited appetite find in emotions of the affective appetite both their origin and term (*ST*, I-II, 25,1).

The Spirited Emotions Are Empowering Emotions

Perhaps the best way to speak of the spirited emotions is to call them enabling or empowering. They empower us to be resolute in our pursuit of the good when difficulty or discouragement causes us to question its goodness. The spirited emotions spring into action to facilitate our quest for the good at exactly those times of temptation and doubt when we begin to suspect the purpose we have set for our life is not worth the struggle attaining it demands. These are the emotions which protect us from abandoning something that is crucial to our well-being. The goodness of what we love dims when obtaining it is hard; something of its original lustre is tarnished when we grow weary of seeking it. At some point in our lives, our good may not look so good any more; thus we wonder if we were initially deceived about its goodness. Sometimes the good is attractive because it is easily had; however, when obtaining it grows difficult we may find it repugnant. Amidst adversity, what we love can seem tremendously unpromising. That such is a common experience explains why we need the spirited emotions. They protect us from disenchantment when achieving our good is toilsome. Aquinas speaks to this when he writes,

It is true that the good is attractive to the affective appetite insofar as it is pleasurable. But insofar as it is difficult to come by, the affective appetite finds it repugnant. Hence the need for another faculty inclining one to take issue with the difficulty. The same thing holds for avoiding evils. Now this is precisely the role of the spirited faculty (*ST*, I-II, 23,2).

Aquinas is being quite realistic about our moral experience. He is also being realistic about the price we must pay for the things we love. It is difficult to follow through on our loves first because all loves are costly, second because there are many things clamoring for our attention that call us away from our love, and third because the quest for anything good takes place among things which oppose us.

For instance, what about those moments in which our zest for a commitment grows stale. It happens in marriages when spouses say their relationship is flat but they are not sure why. It happens in any committed relationship when the energy which inspired the original commitment is diminished. Thomas is also talking about moments of hardship when we find it difficult to accomplish our good because life seems turned against us. The world not only fails to cooperate, it even seems actively to oppose us and we are not sure why. These are moments of adversity, and if they are many they can steal our life away. Too much adversity breaks us down, too much misfortune crushes our spirits. I remember talking once to a woman who was going through a difficult time in her life. Her family was faced with financial problems. Her youngest daughter was very ill. This woman told me not only did she feel she was drowning, she also felt someone was holding her under.

That is a moment of adversity, and for some people it can be so frequent it does not describe just part of their lives, but how they feel about their lives as a whole. These are people for whom evil has become the familiar. They live in the grip of the horrible and it robs them of a normal life. These are people, for instance, who have seen the ravages of war and never quite recovered. These are people for whom life is essentially an experience of violence, the violence of destructive relationships, the violence of unbroken hardship, the violence of injustice. For all of them, evil has become the familiar, crushing their hope, leaving them convinced they cannot achieve the purposes with which they had identified their lives. For Aquinas, this is morally perilous because too much adversity can kill desire, and without desire, as he told us, we do nothing at all. In order to be moral we have to be passionate about something, but passion ebbs in the face of misfortune, and tragedy can quench it altogether.

This is why we need the spirited emotions. They work at those times when we no longer feel what we love is possible for us. Put differently, they work at those times we don't feel like working at all. Hope rescues us from the abyss of despair. Courage saves us from the paralysis of fear. Anger lets us know there is something we cherish enough to fight whatever attacks it. The spirited emotions are secondary inasmuch as their meaning is taken from the affective emotions they serve; however, they are primary inasmuch as they are indispensable ingredients to the moral life. In an ethics of virtue in which the good remains something we seek and into which we grow, courage and hope are crucial as the powers which enable us not to give up in discouragement or surrender to fear. There are many points at which life could have stopped for all of us, moments of terrible suffering, moments of lasting loss, moments of deep cruelty and pain, but if we had stopped we would have died. What empowered us to stumble on at such moments of darkness, Aquinas says, was exactly hope and courage. They strengthened us with resources we did not know we had. They gave us confidence when we thought we were forsaken.

Hope: The Emotion Midway between Love and Joy

It may be good to end this chapter with a word about hope. If we look carefully at the ordering of the emotions, we notice that hope lies midway between love and joy. In a sense, Thomas seems to be saying that hope connects the start of the moral life in love with its completion in joy. Hope is the link between love and joy, because often it is through hope that our love stays alive and moves to fullness. This explains why hope may sometimes be more vividly experienced in our everyday lives than love. Love empowers hope, but love moves through hope unto joy. We believe in a love that stands behind our hope, but sometimes it is hope that keeps love alive; at the very least, it is hope that convinces us our love will not be disappointed.

Hope is certainly a crucial virtue of the moral life. That does not mean it is more important than love, but it does mean that without hope what we love is likely to be lost. Hope respects our human condition as wayfarers. We are pilgrims en route to a promise, a promise we feel but do not yet fully possess. Hope is the virtue that assures us something promising but difficult to attain is nonetheless possible. As Josef Pieper comments, "The virtue of hope is preeminently the virtue of the *status viatoris;* it is the proper virtue of the 'not yet'."[1] According to Pieper, hope urges us to our highest possibility. As a virtue, hope fixes our attention on the best thing that can happen to us—the full assimilation of ourselves in God—and sees this as the only genuine and acceptable fulfillment of ourselves.

The value of hope is in proportion to the good to be lost in despair. If the promise is small, there is little despair kills; however, if the promise is grand, despair is the deadliest of conditions. As we mentioned before, Thomas has a magnanimous ethic, a vision of the moral life that calls us to our most promising possibility. Pieper defines magnanimity as "the aspiration of the spirit to great things," and adds that a "person is magnanimous if he has the courage to seek what is great and becomes worthy of it. . . . Magnanimity . . . decides in favor of what is, at any given moment, the greater possibility of the human potentiality for being."[2] A magnanimous person hungers for grand

and noble possibilities; he or she thirsts for what is best. Magnanimity is a hallmark of Thomistic ethics. His is a morality that consistently aims for what is best for us and refuses, despite whatever obstacles or disappointments, to lower its vision of what God enables and calls us to be. Thomas knows in order to be fulfilled we have to risk something great.

But sometimes despair can be an overpowering temptation. Sometimes the facts of our lives are such that promises of grand possibilities seem farfetched. We would like to believe such hopes, but we are not sure we can. Discouragements choke visions of greatness. Think of what it is like when on account of disappointments sadness settles upon our hearts. It depresses us in the literal sense of weighing us down. It makes it difficult, and sometimes impossible, for us to act. Sadness steals life away. Sadness immobilizes, for it robs us of the hope we need to believe something good is possible. In Aquinas's parlance, too much sadness deadens our belief in God's love. Where the object of hope is great, its loss in despair is tragic.

The term in classical Christian spirituality for such life-robbing sadness is "acedia." Pieper says "acedia is a kind of sadness—more specifically, a sadness in view of the divine good in man. . . . This sorrow is a lack of magnanimity; it lacks courage for the great things that are proper to the nature of the Christian. . . . One who is trapped in acedia has neither the courage nor the will to be as great as he really is."[3]

We see that acedia is a sorrow specifically linked to our greatest possibility. To be oppressed by acedia is to despair of the glory to which God calls us. It is sorrow born from a loss of hope in ever achieving what God's love wants for us. Acedia shrivels our vision of life's possibilities. When its hopelessness starts to control us, the setbacks and defeats of life seem final. No matter how tempting and understandable acedia might be, it is morally and spiritually fatal because, as Pieper concludes, it means "in the last analysis, that man will not be what God wants him to be—in other words, that he will not be what he really is."[4] In Aquinas's schema, acedia is the harvest of despair, for it comes upon the person who no longer believes in the life-enhancing power of God's love. As he explains:

> On the other hand, to look upon some worthwhile good as impossible to achieve, whether alone or with the help of others, stems from extreme depression, which sometimes can dominate someone's affections to the point where he begins to think that he can never again be given aspirations towards

the good. Because acedia is a kind of sadness having this depressive effect upon the spirit, it gives rise to despair (*ST*, II-II, 20,4).

We began this chapter with a story of a woman who found it hard to believe anything worthwhile could be hers. Depression had left her in a dangerous position because she had almost despaired that her life could be other than it was. In order to survive, she had to garner some hope. Though sad, this story helped us appreciate the role of the passions and emotions in the moral life. Each gauges our relationship with what we take to be our sovereign good. Love centers us, desire moves us, joy completes us. But as the story of this woman illustrated, there is also much that saps our love, weakens our desire, and kills our joy. Adversity, misfortune, tragedy, all these breed a sadness of the heart that, if it is not addressed, can be deadly. There must be a way we can deal with these dimensions of the moral life, and through his account of the spirited emotions Aquinas has shown us there is. Courage, hope, and anger are emotions that battle against all that discourages and depresses. They are the powers that steel us against adversity and urge us onward when we are tempted to stop short.

Still, if we are wayfarers en route to God we need more than passion and emotion to survive. We also need virtues. To make our way through a maze of challenges and opportunities, we need a keen sense of how best to respond so that the good gets done and we move forward. To negotiate the moral life, we need to be wise and astute. We need to be morally ingenious. We need to know how to do exactly what needs to be done in all the situations which confront us so that the good does not get lost. Passion is necessary for this, but so is moral skill, and that is how Thomas understood the virtues. The virtues comprise the array of skills necessary to negotiate the moral life successfully. It is through them that we move steadily to our good and gradually fulfill our natures. The virtues are essential to our moral completion. What they mean and how they function is what we shall consider next.

7. The Virtues: Actions That Guide Us to Fullness of Life

One of the more unsettling moral exercises is to consider all the ways a human life can go wrong. It is a sobering meditation, perhaps a chilling one, because it is easy for us to recognize how close we have been to taking turns in our lives that would make us someone other than who we either want or are called to be. It is easy for a human life to go wrong, not because we deliberately choose to make a mess of our lives, but because we can so casually adopt patterns of behavior which can seem incidental, but stretched through the years leave us a lifetime away from where we ought to be. It is disconcerting to have that awareness, to realize one day that we are so far from where we ought to be, but it is possible, and it will happen unless we demonstrate a steady, deliberate resolve to be good.

The virtues see life in epic proportions. There is a promise to life, some beautiful, noble potential, but it has to be achieved and there is no guarantee it will be. Unless we adopt a way of life which nurtures and fashions this promise, then not only will we fall short of it, we shall also become someone other than who in grace we are meant to be. To end up someone other than who we are meant to be—a lifetime away from our promise—is neither difficult nor rare; that is why we need the virtues. We move to our place of belonging through the virtues, through practicing over a lifetime the kinds of activities that will shape us into the greatness Christians call holiness. But that is not easily wrought, and it is not begun at all unless we dedicate ourselves to cultivating the moral skills which enable us to grow in the splendor of our love. Such a transfiguration of ourselves takes practice, commitment, and time, for it is based in the awareness that human wholeness demands becoming so much more than we already are. But we can become less than we already are and we know it. We know we can make of ourselves people we ultimately regret. We know it is possible because at times we have done so. We have caught ourselves in patterns of sinfulness. We have eased into destructive behavior, the harm of which we were hardly aware. We have taken up a pattern of carelessness which is slowly but unerringly debilitating. We have had moments of unusual, if painful, self-awareness when we realized some precious goodness in us had been lost; we had become corrupted. And perhaps what is most disturbing about these moments is that so often we are scarcely aware of how misguided we had become. It begins innocently and unreflectively in a single gesture; however, those single gestures, which seem harmless in themselves can, if they enjoy enough of a history, make us a person of whom we shall be ashamed.

We are capable of our own destruction. Thomas knew this and it is why he fashioned an ethic of virtue. The idea of the virtues comes from a certain conception of a human being as having tremendous capacity for good and for evil. Human beings are creatures who can go to extremes. As an approach to the moral life, the virtues respect our wonderful capacity for goodness, but they also know there is something beautiful and noble in us that can be terribly destroyed, something sacred that can be desecrated, something sublime and graced that can be lost. Here is where we stand in the moral life: we stand poised between possibilities for greatness or awfulness, poised between a promise to be made or destroyed. It is through the virtues that we grow into our promise, and it is through their opposite, the vices, that we slowly dismantle and finally destroy ourselves. This is the picture of the moral life seen through the virtues. We are called to give glory and praise to God, to make of our lives songs of adoration and love, but we know there are pitfalls to this goodness, we know there are many things that can snare us, ways of life that are corrupting and disordering, kinds of behavior that work, not an upbuilding, but a deterioration.

Moreover, though we are called to this goodness there is no assurance we shall achieve it. We can bring ourselves to shame. There is nothing to save us from self-sabotage, nothing to protect us from tearing ourselves down. Nothing determines us to the good and nothing will stop us, if we insist, from making ourselves bad. In the moral life, the only guarantee of goodness is the virtues. The virtues are the actions which enable the upbuilding of ourselves in the good, while the vices are actions too, but are corrupting actions, which vitiate and destroy, actions which work an ongoing deterioration. The virtues make us morally beautiful, the vices make us morally gross.

We are meant to be good, but we can be corrupted. This is the moral realism of Aquinas and it stands behind his argument for the virtues. Thomas has always insisted on the most blessed and promising possibility of our lives; however, precisely because he knows there is something marvelous we can achieve, he also knows there is something wonderful that can be lost. We are balanced between possibilities for greatness or awfulness. We can embrace the gift of our life and move to the fullness of divine love, but we can also squander and destroy this gift. Aquinas calls us to the greatness of charity-friendship with God, for he knows it is only in that kinship with Love that we shall find peace and joy for our souls. We are summoned to journey in charity, to deepen in the love that brings wholeness and fullness of life. But we can refuse that love, we can turn away from it, we can absolutely deny it. We can turn back on the God who calls us to life and try to find life elsewhere. We can, as every sinner knows, try our luck with something other than God. But if we make that choice consistently we shall know only misfortune, for we shall behave in a way that denies us the happiness and joy the heart relentlessly seeks. Virtues are activities which direct us to God, ways of behaving that focus us on the goodness that is the restoration and redemption of our lives. But we can act otherwise, we can choose to be vicious instead of virtuous, evil instead of good.

Our lives are ours to make. Thomas knew this and it is why he pleads with us to become virtuous instead of wicked. What becomes of us is in our hands—we have that noble but dreadful responsibility. We have the capacity to grow in goodness, but we are not destined to it. We have to work to become good, for even if we want to become good, it does not happen naturally or easily for us; it happens only with great effort. That is the insight behind any account of the virtues: we can be something beautiful, noble and good, but we must devote our energies to achieving it. We who are wayfarers make our way back to God through the virtues. We return to God not by change of place, but by change of person, and that is what the virtues achieve. They work the transformation in us that enables our reunion with God.

In this chapter we shall study first why we need the virtues and what they mean (*ST,* I-II, 49, 1–4); second, we shall consider how they are acquired (*ST,* I-II, 51, 1–3), how they grow (*ST,* I-II, 52, 1–3; II-II, 24, 9), but also how they can be lost (*ST,* I-II, 53, 1–3). In the following chapter we shall explore the special relation of every virtue to charity. We shall speak about the cardinal virtues, so indispensable for us to get through life. And finally we shall trace the most stunning paradox in Aquinas's account of the moral life, considering why it is that our virtues reach their perfection in a gift.

I. WHY WE NEED THE VIRTUES AND WHAT THEY MEAN

We need the virtues because we have to do something with the life we have been given. God begins our life with the gift of God's love and, as we shall see, it is God's love that completes it. But in the meantime we have to do something with the gift we have been given—we have to act on God's love, we have to respond to it. We are entrusted with our lives. Our fundamental moral task is to take the gift we have been given and to shape it to completion.

But where does this leave us? If our life stands unfinished, it can go either way. We can pick apart the gift entrusted to us, or we can cradle it to wholeness. In his book, *Between Chaos and New Creation,* Enda McDonagh suggests we are called to move from chaos to "cosmos" or wholeness of life. Taking a hint from the first verse of *Genesis,* McDonagh notes that in the beginning there was not life but chaos, there was not order but the formless void, the abyss of darkness.[1] Chaos represents something not yet brought into being, something not yet formed and shaped into life. If something is chaotic it lacks distinctiveness and identity. To create is to give "cosmos" to chaos, it is to draw life out of the void. When God created the world, God brought form and order and beauty to chaos, God breathed life into the void. With creation, God gave shape to the abyss, God brought something beautiful to be. As McDonagh sees it, with creation God began the movement from chaos to cosmos. But creation stands unfinished. We are called to move from chaos to cosmos, from formlessness to fullness. This is the thrust of creation and our most abiding moral challenge—to overcome chaos by wholeness, to embrace the grace of creation and nurse it to completion. To be moral is to live in a way that enables the triumph of love over the void. A good moral action—a virtue—is one that achieves fuller creation, one that edges us a bit further from chaos. To develop morally is to sustain the transformation God's love began and God's love will complete.

This is why we need the virtues. We stand stretched between the chaos from which we have emerged and the wholeness still to be achieved. This is our moral predicament. We have not yet escaped chaos fully, but we are called through virtuous behavior to loosen the grip of chaos through actions which bring life. We need the virtues to overcome chaos and achieve fullness of life. We are not fully strangers to the void. We know the disorder of sin, we know what it is to slip into darkness. Our predicament throughout the moral life is to stand some-where between chaos and cosmos, to be poised rather precariously between these opposite possibilities. More than likely, we know our-selves as a mix of chaos and cosmos. We are a little bit of virtue and a little bit of vice. The task of the moral life is to live in a way that continually moves us away from chaos to being more deeply rooted in creation.

That is why we need the virtues. They are the kinds of activities which continue the life God's grace began. They shape us in goodness, they transform us in the loveliness of God. They move us closer to the fullness we are meant to enjoy. Through the virtues we sculpt our-selves in goodness and life; however, they are indispensable precisely because the fullness of creation is never assured. If our moral predica-ment is to be poised between chaos and cosmos, then we never fully escape the pull to dissolution. We can act in a way that is morally and spiritually debilitating, we can adopt patterns of behavior that take us back to the void. We call these actions vices because they destroy what the grace of creation intends.

This is the vision of the moral life Thomas beholds. A human life can go two ways. It can move to the fullness of life and of love, or it can crawl back into the darkness. Our actions can deepen the promise of life—they can work for cosmos—or they can frustrate it. We can choose creation, and we do if we act virtuously; or we can choose chaos, and we do if we act viciously. Our lives are speckled with choices for both. Our actions have that power. Moral development takes place through our actions—the virtues tell us that—but moral deterioration takes place through our actions as well. Our behavior can work a disordering or it can work for wholeness. We can act in a way that subdues chaos, or in a way in which our lives truly do become disordered and broken. Obviously, the full return of our self to chaos requires quite a bit of disordered behavior, but it is a possibility, which is why we must take our need for the virtues seriously. Sometimes we do meet people whose lives can best be described as chaotic. These are people whose mode of life seems utterly destructive. They have lost something precious, they are dissipated, they have disfigured the promise of their lives. In religious language, they have succumbed to the power of sin. Sin is any behavior that works chaos in our lives, any behavior which undermines what God's love intends. If a good action moves us to fullness of creation, a bad action begins a process of de-creation. To sin is to crawl back into the darkness. Sin is religious language describing a life moving in the wrong direction, which is why sin de-creates—it dismantles what God's love works to make whole.

The Virtues Are Ways of Fostering Proper Attachments

As these reflections make clear, the necessity of the virtues hinges on the fact that we are capable of being many things, but are called to become one thing—in Aquinas's parlance, we are summoned to be a friend of God. But this does not necessarily happen. It happens only through the development and practice of special habits, which Aquinas calls the virtues. Achieving friendship with God demands giving our life a single-hearted focus. It demands restriction, it calls for certain attachments. In order to grow in charity-friendship with God, which Thomas sees as the purpose and goal of our lives, we need to be attached to some things and detached from others, and to foster a special direction for our lives, and that is what the virtues do; it is in this sense that the virtues involve self-definition. At least initially, the virtues work to diminish possibilities by turning us away from some options and toward other options. The virtues instill a particular direction to our lives so that instead of being undetermined before many things, we are continually determined to one thing, our friendship life with God. The virtues narrow down possibilities so that we can become familiar with the good. The task of the moral life is to achieve a familiarity with the good, if possible even to become experts or "virtuosos" in the good, particularly the unsurpassed goodness of God. Through the virtues we move from being strangers to the good to becoming friends of the good. We move from doing good only sporadically or fortuitously, to doing the good predictably and even easily because we have become good ourselves.

This sounds promising, and it is, but the dramatic tension of the moral life is heightened when we realize we can choose to foster destructive detachments. We can live tragically. We have the option to waste ourselves. We can end up with a life we finally regret. An ethic of virtue emphasizes there is nothing to protect us from bad tendencies except the cultivation of good ones. There is nothing to protect us from destructive inclinations except the development of healthy ones. All of us in some way have a penchant for self-sabotage, little ways we work against wholeness, subtle ways we foster our demise, often when we have least reason to do so. We need the virtues to protect ourselves from the deep human tendency to become something other than good. There is no way to grow in goodness except habitually. For Aquinas, there is no such thing as natural moral goodness, there is only habitual moral goodness, goodness that is achieved through a resolute history of virtuous choices (*ST,* I-II, 49,4). Those who know the demands of becoming good recognize this asceticism to the moral life.

Another way of capturing our need for the virtues is to reflect that a human being is someone called to become more than she or he already is. None of us is yet who we ought to be. We have to grow, we need to develop, sometimes we must drastically change. No matter what we have achieved, we are in many ways incomplete. Regardless of the good we have displayed, standing before the loveliness of God, we know we are never good enough. To be human is to have a promise to fulfill, but this suggests that simply being alive is not being human. Our humanity is something we grow into as we develop the distinctive loveliness to which we are called. In Thomas's vision of the moral life, our humanity is mediated through the virtues, because the more we grow in goodness the more genuinely human we are. Our status in the moral life is that we stand before a grand possibility, but must develop a way of life which enables us to attain it, and that is what the virtues do. The virtues comprise the way of life through which we grow, develop, and change unto wholeness. It is through them that all of us who are one thing become something else, namely holy, lovely and good. At any moment of our lives we fall short of the fullness we need—there is always a gap between ourselves and our completeness—but we grow unto that fullness by practicing the kinds of activities commensurate with its goodness.

These are called the virtues. They are "good making" activities because they take the human nature we have been given and gradually, painstakingly, but assuredly endow us with the character of one who is God's friend. Their opposite are the vices because they give us a different character, they form us in ways contrary to our calling. It would be different if we could not be other than who we are meant to be. A horse can be only a horse, a star has no choice but to be a star, but Thomas knows a human being can be something other than human (*ST,* I-II, 49,4). We can be wicked and brutal and devious, we can destroy our human nature, and this is what the vices do to us. Vices ravage us because they distort and destroy the graced promise of our lives. They are debilitating because they pervert what our human nature is meant to achieve. Each of us is a promise which might be but is not yet. The transition from what might be to what is is the work of the virtues. They are lovely activities because they make us lovely people.

The Virtues Are Habits That Make Us Good

And the reason is because the virtues are habits. To have a habit is to possess a particular quality or characteristic that accrues to a person after having acted a certain way over a period of time. It is repeated activity that develops habits, because the activity endows the person with the quality of the act. Habits represent how someone is qualified, determined or changed by the behavior he or she most customarily displays. Habits capture what our behavior makes of us. Our actions mark us with certain qualities or traits, they identify us in the sense that we become what we most consistently do. It is because Thomas speaks of a virtue as a habit (*ST,* I-II, 49,1) that he can say a virtue shapes not only our acts, but also our selves; it is because virtues are habits, and every habit gives a particular quality to the person who acts, that it is not only our behavior which is virtuous, but we who become virtuous as well.

A habit is an acquired quality. For example, if we ask how we might become just people, Thomas would answer, "By practicing acts of justice." One act of justice does not make a just person; rather, a just person is one who by habitually being just takes on the quality of justice. They are essentially people of justice because by acting justly often enough they have been "qualified" or changed by the essence of justice. As we noted in chapter 1, Thomas sees a very tight connection between what we do and who we become. Ultimately we become what we most consistently do because the quality of our actions passes over into ourselves; hence, the quality of the act eventually becomes a quality of the person who acts. This is why we can say just people are those who have been formed in the quality of justice. Acting justly is a habit in them—it is truly second nature—because they have practiced justice often enough to have become just people. They act justly, not occasionally or haphazardly, but habitually and characteristically—it is what we expect of them—because through their behavior they have been transformed into people of justice. As this example illustrates, the more we tend toward certain activities, the more we are transformed by those activities. Just people act justly because they have "taken on" justice. They have been clothed in justice because the quality of justice is now a quality of the self. They bear the quality of justice, they bespeak it in all their behavior because by habitually seeking justice they have come to embody it. To have any virtue is not only to display it in our behavior, but also to possess it in our selves. We are genuinely virtuous, not only when we perform a virtuous act, but also when we are characterized by the quality of the virtue.

There are two things to note about Aquinas's designation of virtues as habits. First, the virtues change us. When Thomas says a habit represents a "modification of a subject" (*ST,* I-II, 49,2), he captures the essence of virtues. Virtues are transformative activities because through them we take on qualities and characteristics we did not previously have. Virtues develop us, they form us, they give a particular cast and shape to our lives. The effect of a habit is a changed self. If it is a virtuous habit, it is a healthy change of self; but if it is a vice, it is a destructive change of self. But what is most reassuring in Aquinas's designation of the virtues as habits, is that we know we can change. If we are not happy with ourself or with much of our behavior, we do not have to be resigned. We can change for the better, we can grow in healthy and happy ways. If we feel snared in destructive kinds of activities, we are not condemned to them, for we can develop other kinds of habits, and through them take on a new and better self. In this sense, Aquinas's ethic of virtue is immensely reassuring because it helps us understand why there is always hope for improvement in our lives. If the virtues are habits and habits are qualities of ourself, then a change is always possible for us through developing the life-giving activities of the virtues.

Second, not only do the virtues change us, but they also change us in a special way. In Aquinas's language, the virtues modify us, but to modify something "is to make it accord with a standard" (*ST,* I-II, 49,2). What is the standard to which the virtues change us? It is the promised perfection of our lives in God. The standard to which Aquinas refers is the absolute restoration of ourselves in charity-friendship. If a virtue is a quality that changes us, then for Aquinas it must change us not just for the better, but for the best. It is through the virtues that we reach our optimum potential, the fullness of our life in God. Virtues do more than change us, they transform us unto the goodness we need for fullness of life. Virtues make us who human beings are meant to be—it is through them that we fulfill our nature—and as Thomas sees it, if we are meant to be friends of God, then the perfection of that friendship is the work of every genuine virtue. Through the virtues we change unto our most blessed possibility. This is what Thomas means when he says this modification of the person effected by the virtues is "an actualization or bringing to fullness of a subject." What does it mean for us to be brought to fullness? It means we shine in the goodness of God, it means we hint of holiness. Like all the saints, it means we have reached our optimum potential by becoming godly.

This analysis of the virtues as habits which change us into the goodness of our highest possibility helps us understand why they are the middle term between who we are now and who we are called to be. They provide the transition necessary for genuine humanity, the link between who we are at any moment of our lives and who we must become if we are not to fall short of our promise. How do we become the most we can become? Through a lifetime of virtuous behavior. And the reason is that the virtues perfect us by forming us in the goodness of our grandest possibility. We noted before that every action takes its shape from the "end" or purpose it is set to achieve. Virtues are acts that take their shape from the "end" of our life that is friendship with God. That is why they are perfecting, and why the change they produce in us is precisely the one requisite for wholeness. Every act is focused on some end; the focus of charity's virtues is the intimacy we have in friendship with God. We are brought to wholeness through actions which bear the goodness we seek. Virtues born from charity's love are acts which unwaveringly seek God, which is why they are perfecting. The virtues achieve an actualization of our self that corresponds to the purpose of our self. We reach the goal of life through the virtues because it is in them that we are transformed from a child of God into a friend of God. Yes, the virtues modify us, they change us, they make us someone we had not been before, and that is precisely their reassurance. If the focus of the activities of our lives—if their abiding intention—is to seek friendship with God, then precisely such a friend is who we shall become.

Virtues achieve the change of self necessary for happiness, and that is because they do not change us haphazardly or superficially; rather, they change us unto God in the deepest, most personal way: they fashion in us a new and blessed self. This is what Thomas means when he writes, "Speaking of habits of soul and body, Aristotle says that they are activity-directed dispositions whose possessor has reached the term of its development; and he goes on to explain that something is fully developed 'if it is disposed in accordance with its nature' " (*ST,* I-II, 49,2). Through the virtues we are brought to the "term of [our] development" because our highest and most fitting development is the transformation of ourself into a person of holiness and love, and it is this the virtues achieve. The optimum development for a human being is not to be wealthy or famous or powerful, but to be a presence of God's love and goodness in the world. Charity's virtues make us that kind of person; they promise and effect that blessed development. Indeed we are "fully developed" through the virtues, because it is by developing and practicing those good-making habits that we accomplish the intended fullness of our nature. As God sees human nature, the most we can possibly be is to be for God the friend God has always been for us. That is the promise intended by the gift of creation, and it is exactly that grace the virtues seize and nurse to fullness.

II.　HOW THE VIRTUES ARE GAINED
AND LOST

Anyone who has tried to develop patience or to practice forgiveness or to be more generous, knows that developing virtue takes time. One act does not a virtue make. Two, three or four acts do not a virtue make. Developing virtue requires repeated action, a history of acting a certain way long enough until the quality of the virtuous act becomes a characteristic of a now virtuous person (*ST,* I-II, 51,2). At first all of us are clumsy and inept with being good because we are not yet familiar enough with a virtue for it to be second nature to us. That is what the virtues do to us, they give us a "second nature" in the sense that they work on and develop the nature, temperament or personality with which we were born. They knead that personality, shaping and forming it in special goodness; they take what we have been given and endow it with virtuous qualities. But like any masterpiece, it takes time for the virtues to shape us into people of good character. The virtues are an argument in how hard it is to become good. We become good not instantly, but with practice, with the painstaking repetition of the kinds of actions capable of transforming us from people who can be good to people who truly are good. As Thomas sees it, each of us has an inclination to the good—we have an initial capacity for virtue, which is why he says we possess the virtues "inchoatively"—but that inclination has to be developed into a habit. Developing a virtue is a matter of taking a tendency and strengthening it into a habit. A virtuous person is one who has developed a potential for goodness, taking a capacity for good behavior and honing it into a stable, predictable skill. All of us from time to time may do good, but if we only occasionally are good, or if we are good only by chance and not by habit, then we have not yet become a virtuous person. Someone who is virtuous does the good characteristically—it is what we expect of them—because they have practiced the good long enough to have become good themselves. Their goodness is not incidental, it is a mark of who they are. This is why Thomas says a virtue makes both an act and the person good.

Initially there is a strangeness to doing good because we are not yet good ourselves. At first we are stutterers in the good; we need the virtues to become eloquent with goodness. But this takes time. Consider how difficult it can be to make compassion second nature to us. Becoming good is a matter of practicing goodness for a long time, at least long enough so that the quality of the good act, whether that be

compassion, patience, justice or forgiveness, becomes a quality of ourselves. For this to happen, Thomas says, "the active element [must]
completely master the passive element" (*ST*, I-II, 51,3). The "passive
element" represents what we potentially can become; it is our capacity
for virtue. The "active element" is the quality of a particular virtue
that must "act on" us, that must carve its special goodness into our
person so that eventually we embody the virtue. When that occurs, we
act justly or temperately or generously because the qualities of those
acts are also characteristics of ourselves.

Too, when Thomas says we only possess a virtue when the quality
of the virtuous act "completely masters" us, he reminds us that a
virtue is something fixed and firm. We are not virtuous if a quality of
goodness is fickle; no, we are virtuous only when our goodness is predictable. A single just act begins the formation of justice within us, but
it is hardly enough to imbue us with the quality of justice. Thomas
sometimes uses the image of water dripping on a rock. Just as it takes
years for water to leave an impression on a rock, so too can it take
years for a virtuous act to impress us with a virtuous quality. Only
little-by-little do we acquire a virtue, as ever so slowly the quality of
the good act imprints in us the quality of goodness itself, transforming
us from a person who can do good to a person who will do good because
he or she is good. When we have the habit of doing good we are a
virtuous person. We are not virtuous in a complete and unqualified
sense until we perform acts of justice, mercy, compassion or forgiveness not only characteristically, but also with a certain pleasure and
ease; thus, a virtuous person does the good not because she is con-
strained to it, but because she embodies goodness—she enjoys doing
good because she enjoys being herself. In Aquinas's language, we possess a virtue when we tend toward its goodness "commonly and
naturally."

Developing a Virtue Often Means Overcoming a Vice

A further reason acquiring virtue is difficult is that so often to
develop a virtue means a vice must be overcome. Thomas suggests this
when he observes one reason it is hard to grow in virtue is that the will
is turned "to many incompatible things" and thus virtue must work
not only to imbue us with goodness, but also to "gradually erode the
opposing conditions" of goodness (*ST*, I-II, 51,3). Those opposing
conditions are many. It is our inclination to evil, it is the presence of
unhealthy, destructive tendencies, it is the stubborn power of vices
which resist the development of virtues. At least initially, the primary

work of virtue may be the toilsome task of uprooting a vice. We need to develop good habits because we have bad habits of which we need to be rid. Virtues are habits which turn us to the good, but vices are habits too; they are bad habits which turn us away from goodness. Virtues are enabling, vices are disabling. Virtues upbuild us, vices corrupt us.

At first, the virtues work a rehabilitation, they struggle to heal a personality broken and wounded by debilitating behavior, and this may comprise a large portion of our moral history. If vice corrupts, virtue renovates, shaping us in goodness by first healing us from evil. Virtues do not work on virgin soil—they work to heal a personality already wounded by sin. It is not as if the virtues appear where nothing was before, for indeed most often acquiring a virtue means overcoming a contrary disposition. And this is not easy. Vices do not die easily, and the reason is that like the virtues they are habits, ingrained tendencies to act a certain way. Vices resist virtue. Because they are habits, they actively seek to overcome any opposing tendencies. We know this in our experience. One reason it is hard to develop patience is that being quick-tempered is a vice, and because it is a vice it is a predictable, firmly lodged way of acting. Or take generosity. Generosity is slowly gained where a stingy spirit once prevailed. Or forgiveness is only painstakingly had where one has been inclined to hardness of heart. These are all the "opposing conditions" to which Aquinas refers. Acquiring virtue takes time because so many vices must be dislodged. To establish virtue, good habits must overcome bad habits, and bad habits do not willingly die.

We may, for example, have a bad habit of gossiping, a bad habit of holding grudges, a bad habit of eating or drinking too much. These are all vices, ingrained, habitual ways of acting, and the longer they have characterized us the deeper in us they have grown. It is not easy to change bad behavior because vices are habits too; they enter us, they become part of our personality. If the quality of a good act passes over into us and leaves its mark, a quality of a bad act leaves its mark too. If virtue works, vice does too. Vice works to overcome and destroy virtue; it is the nature of a habit. Vices are entrenched, and struggle to survive because they are habits. They are not passive before virtue, they are active, fiercely opposing whatever works to silence them. For every virtue there is its opposite working to overcome it.

This helps us understand why it can be so difficult to change behavior, or why it is so maddeningly hard to uproot one habit for the sake of nurturing another one. It also explains why initially our virtue is flickering. In the early stages of its development, all virtue is in danger of being snuffed out by vices, and the reason is that the vices, because they are more firmly developed, are much more powerful than the virtues. If virtues are powers to do good, vices are powers to do evil. Vices resist virtues, they fight being overcome and destroyed by goodness. Vices struggle to survive, which is why we can be easily discouraged in the early stages of our moral development. There is much in us that must be burned away, purged and cleansed before virtue can flourish.

There is moral realism here. Thomas paints a picture of our lives locked in a struggle between good and evil. Each of us is a mixture of both. Morally speaking, a war is being waged in our hearts. It is a war between virtue and vice, a war to see which will prevail in us. We have a disposition to virtue, but we also have a disposition to vice. We develop some virtues, but we know we have developed vices as well. None of us is completely virtuous, but are at least partially controlled by vice. Aquinas's image is of a moral subject under fire. On the one hand, there are virtuous dispositions in us which empower our growth in the good; on the other hand, this progress in virtue is subverted by all those forces in us—Thomas calls them vices—which threaten to pull us down, discourage us, and finally destroy us. Vices work to vitiate the goodness we may have already attained, which is why the development of one bad habit usually signals the erosion of goodness elsewhere in our lives. The moral life stands in tension. To grow in virtue is to be pried free of vice. We stand somewhere in between, hopefully moving toward virtue, but feeling strongly the pull of vice.

The fact that virtue is acquired only with effort suggests that most often taking on a good habit means uprooting and destroying a bad one. Virtues move in where vices used to be. Justice works against selfishness, temperance against debasement, courage against cowardice and recklessness. We are a mix of tendencies, a blend of conflicting forces. Virtues always have opposites, and their opposites are the vices. Vices make virtues necessary, but they also help us understand why we sometimes feel so deeply a contradiction at the heart of our lives, a sort of interior division; even when we strive to be good, do we not still feel the power and hold of sin? It is not surprising then that we can be easily discouraged in our efforts to be good. Why is it that we sometimes are brought down by things we thought we had left behind? We find ourselves being petty or petulant and are surprised because we thought we had developed graciousness. The reason may be that all these negative qualities might be more deeply a part of us than we expected. If they were habitual enough to have become vices, their death will come slowly; and sometimes when we think they are finally purged from us they suddenly reassert themselves, which might explain why our sinfulness so often catches us off guard. These opposite tendencies are set deeply within us, and they are neither passive nor inert. As we grow in virtue we do lessen the hold of sin upon our lives, but if sin is a habit of being it is likely that some trace of it will survive.

The Growth of the Virtues in Us

Aquinas captures the episodic nature of the virtues when he says there are three stages to the acquisition of the virtues. There are the virtues of beginners, the virtues of those already on their way, and the virtues of those who have finally arrived (*ST,* II-II, 24,9). In the first stage, virtue works not so much to do good, but to overcome bad. Here the energy of virtue is directed to uprooting and overpowering vices. In this initial stage of developing virtue, Thomas says the individual must "devote himself mainly to withdrawing from sin and resisting the appetites, which drive him in the opposite direction to charity. This is the condition of beginners, who need to nourish and carefully foster charity to prevent its being lost" (*ST,* II-II, 24,9). In this first stage of our history with virtue, a rehabilitation takes place. A nature wounded and weakened by sin tries to gain strength in the good; this is one reason we said so much of our moral life takes the form of a healing. In the second stage, Thomas says "a man's chief preoccupation is to advance in virtue. This is the mark of those who are making progress, and who are principally concerned that their charity should grow and become strong" (*ST,* II-II, 24,9). Here a virtue's energy is directed to doing good more than resisting evil, but in this second stage we are still apprentices in the life of virtue, slowly learning our way, often doing good falteringly, and having to watch carefully the example of those more practiced in goodness. In this second stage we are trying to grow in the virtues we have acquired, to strengthen their hold in our lives, living in a way that enables us to participate more deeply in a virtue's goodness. In this second stage we work to root ourselves more completely in a virtue, we strive to be possessed by its goodness so that we begin to practice it with facility and delight. To be sure, this second stage comprises the bulk of our moral life. Finally, the third stage of the virtuous life marks those who have "fully arrived." As Aquinas explains, "The third stage is when a man applies himself chiefly to the work of cleaving to God and enjoying him, which is characteristic of the perfect who long to depart and to be with Christ" (*ST,* II-II, 24,9).

Aquinas's delineation of the virtuous life into stages assures us that, however difficult, we can make progress in the moral life. We can grow in goodness; however painfully, we can overcome vice. It may be the struggle of a lifetime, but the harvest of that struggle is the conversion of ourselves into people of true goodness. No matter how difficult growing in justice, forbearance, generosity or compassion might be, the virtues tell us we can take on these qualities the more we practice these acts. Doing good makes us good, that is what an ethic of virtue assures us. We can move beyond who we are now to who we want to be. We sense this when we look back over our lives and spot undeniable changes. We take comfort that we are not now who we once were. Hard work has made us more generous, more compassionate, less selfish, more tolerant, maybe less judgmental. None of this happened naturally, but happened "virtuously" as we strove to nurture tendencies to generosity, compassion, justice and tolerance into virtues of generosity, compassion, justice and tolerance.

The growth of a virtue is measured by a person's possession of that virtue. To have a virtue is to be qualified by its goodness; thus, a virtue grows in us the more we possess the quality of its distinctive goodness. It is not, for example, as if the virtue of justice grows by justice being added to justice; rather, justice grows by us becoming more just persons. A virtue grows as we grow into its goodness. This is why Thomas says the virtues grow not "extensively" but "intensively," which means they grow "not through the addition of one form to another, but through the subject's possessing to a greater or lesser degree one and the same form" (*ST*, I-II, 52,2). A virtue increases in us the more we are rooted in its goodness, the more its special quality becomes a lasting characteristic of ourselves. This is why Thomas says a virtue grows in us in the same way that a tree grows when its roots stretch deeper into the soil. In short, we know a virtue is growing in us when there is increasingly less discrepancy between the goodness of the virtue and the goodness of ourselves.

Why There Is No Limit to Virtue's Growth in Us

At the same time, since the measure of a virtue's goodness is in God and not ourselves, we know there is no limit to how a virtue can grow in us. Virtues reach for the ultimate enhancement of the person, and that means they strive to make us good as God is good. Charity's virtues always admit of more. We can grow in goodness, but we can never exhaust goodness. We can become better, but we can never become best, for that sublime goodness is reserved for God. The measure of a virtue is the goodness it strives to achieve, and for Christians formed in charity's virtues that is the goodness of God. This is what Aquinas means when he says "the exemplar of human virtue ... preexists in God ..." (*ST*, I-II, 61,5). The measure of Christian virtues is the God whose goodness is the perfection of every virtue. This is why even though we may become better, God is always best; it is also why the work of virtue is forever undone. Given the goodness of God, we shall, in some way, always fall short of the goodness we seek. At no point can we say, "Enough!" for definitive goodness resides not in ourselves, but in God. We can always become better; there is no limit to a virtue's growth in us. Virtues whose purpose is to achieve likeness to God can always develop further. We are perfectly virtuous only when there is no discrepancy between who we are and the goodness we need to be; however, when that goodness is divine we know there can be no limit to a virtue's growth. Virtue is identified not in the possessor, but in the goodness the virtue seeks. If virtues formed from charity are identified in God, then we can never stop growing in those virtues because their perfect meaning lives not in ourselves but in God, and although God is a goodness we can approach and come to resemble, God is never a goodness we can equal or surpass.

Put differently, it is not our understanding of goodness that defines a virtue's meaning, it is God's. Christian virtues are defined from God, for their meaning is determined by the goodness they have to attain. Our possession of a virtue marks a stage in our familiarity with the good, but because that goodness is God's, the goodness we have achieved is always something we are summoned to surpass. The meaning of the virtues changes for us as our likeness to God increases. The deeper we grow in a virtue the more we come to understand and embody its perfection which is definitively displayed in God. The nearer we are to God in goodness, the more we come to understand what God sees a virtue to be. The boundary of virtue is established by God. The deeper we grow in charity-friendship with God, the more our own limited understanding of goodness is stretched, surpassed, broken through, and even revolutionized. For instance, we know the virtue of justice means we must give everyone his or her due. But what does this entail? At first we may conclude the most rudimentary justice is to divide things fairly, and that is true. But what happens to justice when it is modeled, not on how we understand fairness, but on the justice of God? Here we begin to think of justice in terms of generosity and compassion and forgiveness, for in God's eyes these are due people as well. With the Christian virtues—virtues modeled on the goodness of God—generosity, compassion and forgiveness are not something other than justice, but justice more perfectly understood.

They capture the essence of justice because they more clearly represent what God takes justice to be.

How Virtue Can Be Lost

To share in the goodness of God captures the utmost possibility of a virtue; but a goodness so carefully gained can be gradually destroyed. Virtues can be lost, and for Aquinas, not surprisingly, they are lost by cultivating any behavior which opposes their particular goodness. Courage is lost when we become either brash or cowardly. Justice is lost through selfishness, the wisdom of prudence is weakened through acts of moral foolishness. A virtue is weakened and destroyed by practicing opposite habits, for indeed the more we do so we unearth the quality of goodness and replace it with the quality of vice. Aquinas puts this succinctly: "Habits are strengthened by the same causes as produce them; in a similar way, habits are weakened by the same causes as destroy them; because the weakening of a habit is the beginning of its destruction, just as the production of a habit is the beginning of its growth" (*ST,* I-II, 53,2).

All Thomas means by this is that if a particular action makes a virtue, its corresponding opposite destroys that virtue and nurtures a vice. That is how the virtues are most commonly lost. By acting contrary to a virtue, the goodness of the virtue is picked apart by the evil of the vice, and if the vice is practiced long enough the virtue will eventually be destroyed; where virtue once thrived, a vice will be flourishing. The evil of the vice erodes and finally destroys the goodness of the virtue. At first the virtue is only weakened, but if the vice remains active the virtue will be destroyed because the "form" of the virtue cannot endure the "form" of the vice. We cannot take our goodness for granted; nor can we grow too comfortable with the virtue we have achieved. Virtues have to be practiced to remain strong. Thomas touches here on the danger of becoming morally complacent or careless. In the moral life, sloppiness takes its toll and brings more harm than we expect. To grow lazy in virtue is to begin virtue's deterioration. Being as good as we can is not a moral platitude. In a virtue ethic it is a moral necessity, for not to practice the virtues we have is to open ourselves to the vices we never completely lose.

We began this chapter with the comment that our lives are ours to make. Something splendid is entrusted to us, but it can be destroyed. A human life can be wasted, which is why we must grow in virtue and strive to avoid vice. To act virtuously is to respond in kind to the love that has created us. Our life begun in grace is called to glory. How do we move to glory? One way is to become people of virtue, because by acquiring the virtues we undergo the transformation in ourself necessary for blessedness with God. The virtues guide us to fullness of life because they make not only our actions good, they make us good. By developing good habits, we take on the qualities of goodness itself; the virtues change our character. We know this is not easy because we have also spent time with the vices, and they are habits too; however, the grand consolation of an ethic of virtue is that we can make progress in the moral life. The virtues tell us we can change, they assure us possibilities for goodness are always open to us.

But can we ever be good enough? We close with the reflection that virtues which seek God are measured by the goodness of God. One thing this means is that there can be no limit to virtue's growth in us because their ultimate meaning is displayed not in ourselves but in God. But does it also mean that we forever fall short of the goodness we need to be redeemed? It would seem so. There is a further twist to Aquinas's account of the virtues. Not only does he describe the virtues in a way that to grow in them is to grow in openness to God; he also suggests that our virtue inherently lacks the goodness we need to gain God. Is Aquinas setting us up? Does his account of the moral life begin promisingly but end in futility and absurdity? The key to answering these questions lies in fathoming the special connection between charity and the other virtues for Aquinas. But it also lies in recognizing how important it is for Aquinas that the virtues reach their perfection in the Gifts of the Spirit. We shall consider all this in chapter 8. It should be clear then that what begins in a gift needs to be brought to glory, but our glory is a matter of a gift as well.

8. The Virtues: Finding Our Perfection in a Gift

The vision behind Aquinas's moral theology is our reunion with God. How do we return to our place of belonging? This has been the question driving Aquinas's vision of the moral life. If we are created from love, how do we return to love? We do so by loving, by centering our lives in charity and making that passionate, heartfelt love of God the abiding intention of our lives. If friendship for God burns in our hearts, everything we do bespeaks it. If charity is our sovereign love, every other action lives at its service. This is why Thomas understood the virtues to be strategies of charity's love. They do not work apart from charity, they work for the sake of charity. Formed in the crucible of its love, charity directs all our activity to God. In this chapter we shall first explore the relation between charity and the other virtues, paying special attention to what it means to say every virtue is formed from charity's love and why there can be no true virtue without charity (*ST*, II-II, 23, 6–8). We shall also examine four other virtues Thomas says are essential for successfully negotiating the moral life. He calls these the cardinal virtues. What they are and how they are related to charity will also be part of our discussion (*ST*, I-II, 57, 4–5; 61, 3; II-II, 123, 4–6; 141, 2–4; 144, 2, 4; 145, 1).

But is charity enough to gain reunion with God? Thomas says no. God is the goodness constitutive of happiness, but God is also a goodness forever beyond us. Try as we might, we shall never be good enough to gain God. Through the virtues we grow in the goodness of God, but we can never equal or surpass that goodness. This is what makes Aquinas's ethic of virtue different. It emphasizes our responsibility for the gift of life entrusted to us, but it also appreciates keenly our limitations. Even if we lived a perfectly virtuous life, we could not gain God through our goodness. Though eminently virtuous, we still depend on God's love to do for us what our love cannot.

This is why Aquinas's schema of the moral life begins in grace and ends in gift. From first to last, it is God's love that enables us. It is the gift of God's love poured out in our hearts that begins the moral life for us and enables us to respond to God at all; but it is also the gift of God's love in the Spirit that completes our virtue and leads us home. For Aquinas, it is God who seizes our virtues and perfects them, which is why he says charity's virtues blossom in the Gifts of the Spirit. Charity's virtues end where our moral life began, in God's passionate, gracious love for us. From first to last, all is grace. This, too, we shall consider by studying Thomas's account of the Gifts of the Spirit and why they are the perfection of virtues born from charity (*ST,* I-II, 68, 1–4; 70, 3). Though seldom noted in most studies of Thomistic ethics, it is in the Gifts of the Spirit, not the virtues, that the moral life finds its completion for Thomas, and it will be important for us to see why. But first let us examine what Thomas means when he says every virtue must be born from charity's love.

I.   CHARITY AND THE OTHER VIRTUES

We have hinted already that in Aquinas's schema of the Christian moral life there is a special relationship between all the virtues and charity. Aquinas argued there could "be no true virtue without charity" (*ST,* II-II, 23,7), and the reason is that a virtue fulfills its purpose only if it helps us achieve the ultimate goal of our lives, which for Aquinas was friendship with God. To satisfy the definition of virtue, any virtue must be the kind of activity which enables us to achieve our most promising good. Virtues dispose us to our maximum achievement, which is why to understand them we must see them in connection to the goal they are set to achieve. Virtues take their meaning from the purpose they serve. We only know what a virtue means when we ask, "A virtue for what?" Whatever we take to be our ultimate goal gives shape and substance to the virtues. Virtues are activities that make us good, but we only know what that means when we have some account of what a good life is for us and what a good life seeks.

It is this notion of a good life that governs the meaning of the virtues. We can fully understand what a virtue is only when we have some understanding of human excellence. To identify a virtue we must look first not at the virtue itself, but at the good the virtue serves. Different en ls, different purposes, different understandings of human excellence will call for different understandings of virtue. It is what we take to be our ultimate goal which determines what a virtue needs to be. This is why all of us can talk about the virtues but not mean the same thing by them. We may speak about justice and courage, but our agreement may extend no further than the names we give those virtues.[1] If we have different understandings of what counts for excellence, we will disagree sharply over what constitutes the substance of justice, courage or any other virtue. How we understand a virtue turns on how we understand the most fitting purpose of our lives. A virtue functions to relate us to the goal that is our happiness and perfection, and for Christians it is charity-friendship with God. Thomas knew there had to be a close relationship between charity and all the virtues, because for him something was only a virtue if through its practice our friendship with God was deepened and sustained. Virtues formed in charity's love ought to enable us to touch our ultimate possibility in every area of our lives. It is because they do so that they are truly perfecting activities. Thomas explains,

> It is obvious then that true virtue, without any qualification, is directed to our principal good; as Aristotle puts it, virtue is "what disposes a thing already perfectly constituted in its nature to its maximum achievement." And so taken, there can be no true virtue without charity (*ST*, II-II, 23,7).

What is it about charity that empowers every other virtue to its optimum achievement? Thomas says it is because if friendship with God is the sovereign intention of our lives, then everything we do will be born from its love. This is what he means when he speaks of charity as the "form" of all the virtues. Charity is the love informing and influencing and shaping and directing all virtuous activity. If we recall what Thomas said about the power of our most persistent intentions, we know if some intention holds sway in our lives it is efficacious in all we do. Our primary desire expresses itself in our behavior. If through charity we really do seek God in all things, then that desire directs to God everything we do. If charity is the sovereign love of our lives, then all our actions, however small, will have supernatural bearing.

Aquinas sometimes captures the relationship between charity and the other virtues by speaking of charity as the "mother" of the virtues. As he explains, "Charity is called the end of the other virtues because it directs them all to its own end. And since a mother is one who conceives in herself from another, charity is called the mother of the other virtues, because from desire of the ultimate end it conceives their acts by charging them with life" (*ST*, II-II, 23,8).

Aquinas uses this image to show that every virtue is conceived from charity's love. As a mother gives birth to her child, charity gives birth to all genuinely virtuous behavior. We can understand this if we remember that, for Aquinas, charity is not only a single virtue, but is the comprehensive activity of our lives. Charity describes not only a kind of behavior, but constitutes a particular kind of life. It is in this sense that charity is the life activity from which all we do is born. Every virtue is given life in the crucible of friendship with God. That is why each virtue is formed from charity's love and achieves charity's perfection. Every virtue is quickened by charity. And every virtue is intrinsically connected to charity because each emerges from within the life of charity itself; it is the ongoing friendship we have with God that gives each virtue its most fitting expression. This does not mean that every virtue ultimately is charity, but that nothing can be a virtue if it is not the work of our friendship life with God. To be a virtue truly, an act has to be formed from within that friendship, express it, and seek it. Charity mothers the virtues because each virtue comes to life as an expression of the intimacy we have with God; each virtue is the creation of that love life.

The Cardinal Virtues

Nonetheless, even though charity is indispensable in the moral life, it is not sufficient. Thomas lists other primary virtues, among them the four cardinal virtues: prudence, justice, temperance, and fortitude or courage. As the name suggests, these virtues form the "hinge" or "axis" on which the moral life turns. What does Thomas mean? Why are these virtues so prominent in his schema of the moral life? These are the virtues we need to get through life. Without them we will not be able to sustain our journey to the good. If we are to make progress in the moral life, we must be prudent, just, temperate and courageous; these are the qualities we need to get by, the virtues required to navigate successfully all the challenges of the moral life.

Aquinas calls these the cardinal virtues because every virtue—except the theological virtues of faith, hope and charity—is in some way derived from them and in some way manifests them. The cardinal virtues express some aspect or ingredient of every virtue, so that every virtue shows itself in some way as prudence, in some way as justice, in some way as temperance and fortitude. The cardinal virtues mark four general conditions or qualifications an act must have if it is to be virtuous. If an act is a virtue, we must be able to look at it from one perspective and see prudence, from another perspective we must spot justice, from a third we should recognize temperance, and from a fourth courage or steadfastness should be displayed. The cardinal virtues capture how each virtue is seen from a certain angle. In other words, insofar as any act is a virtue, it is also prudence, justice, temperance, and fortitude. In order for an act to be virtuous, we must be able to look at it and see each of these four qualities at work.

As Aquinas sees it, every virtuous act will be composed of these four elements. If something is virtuous, it is prudent inasmuch as it is right judgment about what needs to be done; it is just insofar as it does what needs to be done in the way it needs to be done; it is temperate because it displays the right amount of passion or energy in the doing of good—the act flows from a well-ordered affection; and it is courageous because it is not deterred by fear or hardship. Something of these four qualities enters into the definition of every virtue. This is how Thomas describes the cardinal virtues and their relationship to a virtuous act:

> Thus they are called principal as being common to all virtues. For instance, any virtue that causes a good judgment of reason may be called prudence; every virtue that causes actions to fulfill what is right and due may be called justice; every virtue that restrains and tames the passions may be called temperance; every virtue that strengthens the mind against any onset of passion may be called fortitude. . . . It is in this way that the other virtues are contained under them (*ST*, I-II, 61,3).

The Primacy of Prudence

The most important cardinal virtue is prudence. What is its role? Because a virtue is a characteristic way of acting, we can sometimes think that it refers to rote, mechanical ways of behaving, almost as if virtue overrides any ingenuity or flexibility in human behavior. But that is not so. A virtue is a moral skill that enables a person to fathom in all the situations which confront her, precisely how the good can be done or needs to be done. Ethics is a practical science, which deals with concrete, everyday behavior. But given the vast array of human situations, it is very hard to predict in advance exactly how the good ought to be done. Rules and guidelines help us, but they cannot always tell us exactly what needs to be done. That requires discernment and wisdom, and this is what prudence supplies. Prudence comes first in

the formation of every virtuous act because prudence is right judgment about what needs to be done.

We can appreciate this if we think back on certain situations in
our lives in which we concluded that following a rule would not allow
us to achieve the moral good; in that instance, there was something
about the principle or rule that did not adequately address what confronted us. It is in such moments that we feel the need for prudence. A
virtuous person is one who can see what a situation requires and enables. She knows the more concrete and particular a situation becomes, the harder it is to know what ought to be done simply by
following a rule. Some discernment is required. We must be able to see
the situation for what it is, respecting its unique dimensions. We must
grasp what it means to be good at this time and place, recognizing
what might be special about a particular situation.

This is the work of prudence. For Aquinas, there could be no
possibility of virtue without prudence. No matter how well-inten-
tioned, if we were not prudent we could not be virtuous. Aquinas described prudence as "right judgment" about what needs to be done.
Ethics is a practical science and prudence is practical wisdom. Prudence is the moral skill to know what needs to be done in the situation
before us and how to do it. "What shape must the good take in this
situation if I am not to fall short of achieving it?" That is the question
of prudence, it strives to figure how we must act if we are not to misfire
in our desire to do good. When we are in a situation in which there are
many possibilities for action, a prudent person discerns what best
enables the flourishing of the good. Prudence is a virtue of moral
discernment, which reads the situation to glean from all its ingredients exactly how best to achieve the good. Sometimes it discerns the
single way the good must be done if the good is not to be lost. It is a
virtue of moral astuteness that helps us see more clearly how the good
is fittingly practiced so our intentions do not fall short. Not a virtue of
caution or restraint, prudence gives ingenuity to our love.

At one point in the *Summa,* Aquinas says, "Prudence is necessary, not merely that a man may become good, but so that he may lead
a good life" (*ST,* I-II, 57,5). The image here is of having to make our
way through all sorts of situations in which various responses will be
appropriate. Each situation calls us to do good, but because the situations are different, they call us to achieve the good in different ways.
That is why there is an artistry to being virtuous. Doing the good is
never a matter of rote, mechanical behavior; rather, doing good rests
on the ability to discern exactly what shape the good must take so that
we don't falter. The image here is of motion, of journeying through life

amidst a variety of challenges, of navigating our way through all sorts
of situations as we travel to God. We make our way through prudence,
which is the moral wisdom we need if we are not to be undone on our
journey. As Aquinas summarizes, "Prudence is necessary not merely
that a person may become good, but so that he may lead a good life"
(*ST,* I-II, 57,5).

Even charity is not enough for the virtuous life. It is preeminent
and essential, but it is not sufficient. Charity needs to be guided by
prudence. In morals, good intentions are not enough. With charity we
have the best of intentions—we want to direct all our actions towards
God—but we must also know how to make good on that intention, and
such is the work of prudence. We may want the right things, but
sometimes we do not know how to achieve the good we intend. We
may have wonderful intentions, but be inept at carrying them out. The
virtue of prudence counsels us on how best to make good on our intentions. It is a kind of executive ability which enables us to see concretely how the good can be done. A prudent person knows how to find
the right means for a good end, they know how to put ends and means
together. The necessity of prudence in the virtuous life reminds us it is
not enough to know and desire the good; we must also be astute
enough to see how to achieve the good. With prudence, we gain the
moral wisdom we need to know how to act if the good is not to be
denied.

And yet, even though charity needs prudence to bring a certain
wisdom or ingenuity to our love, prudence, like all the virtues, is at the
service of charity. Prudence is moral wisdom with a specific focus. Its
interest is knowing how to act so that we can accomplish the basic
intention of our lives, that of being friends of God. Aquinas captures
the relationship between prudence and charity when he says, "Prudence is of good counsel about matters regarding a man's life in its
entirety, and its last end. . . . Those only are such who are of good
counsel about what concerns the whole of human life" (*ST,* I-II, 57,4).

Prudence grasps how to achieve the overriding concern of our
lives in our everyday behavior. It is moral wisdom not only about the
particular action before us, but also about our lives taken as a whole.
More precisely, prudence knows how to make that particular act serve
the overall purpose of charity-friendship; in fact, it is precisely in
achieving this that it enables our concrete behavior to be truly virtuous. Standing in the service of charity, there is a special vision to
prudence. If charity needs the moral acuity of prudence, prudence
always has charity in mind. It is not a stodgy virtue, not a virtue of
caution or restraint; on the contrary, prudence looks through the im-

mediate to the ultimate, and reads the everyday in the light of the future we want our behavior to achieve. A prudent act is not short-sighted, but visionary, because it always has the Kingdom in view. Prudence guards against moral myopia, it fights any narrowing of vision by which we lose sight of the Kingdom charity seeks. Prudence stretches and challenges us, and goads us to remember that a truly virtuous act always seeks to resemble the goodness of God. Far from being restrictive, prudence insists that every act be as good as it possibly can.

The second cardinal virtue is justice. We can treat it briefly. If prudence is the ability to know what needs to be done, justice is doing what needs to be done in the way it needs to be done. What distinguishes justice from prudence is that prudence is understanding what needs to be done—it is right judgment—and justice is doing what needs to be done—it is right action (*ST,* I-II, 61,4). Prudence discerns, justice enacts.

Courage and Temperance: Dealing with What Obstructs Virtue

The cardinal virtues of temperance and fortitude are related. Both pertain, not directly to actions, but to impediments of action. Their focus is the emotions, particularly when the emotions, instead of aiding the doing of good, make doing good difficult. Thomas sees this happening in two ways. One is if we are tempted to turn from the good because of fear or difficulty. It is in such moments that we need the virtue of courage to enable us "to be steadfast and not turn away from what is right" (*ST,* I-II, 61,3). We have already discussed the importance of courage in our analysis of the passions and emotions. We know we need courage whenever adversity confronts us. We know sometimes we are discouraged in doing good because life is hard. We suffer setbacks, we are victims of bad luck, we know the scourge of misfortune. There are periods of darkness, times, as Faulkner writes in *The Sound and the Fury,* when "life looks like pieces of a broken mirror." Courage gives us the resolve we need to do the good amidst adversity. Aquinas quotes Augustine who said that "courage is 'love readily enduring all for the sake of what is loved' " (*ST,* II-II, 123,4). Given the temptation to flee the good when doing it is threatening or hard, it is not surprising that Aquinas says "the chief activity of courage is not so much attacking as enduring, or standing one's ground amidst dangers" (*ST,* II-II, 123,6). To have courage is to persevere in times of hardship for the sake of what we love and do not want to lose.

It may be useful to discuss temperance in more detail, for it is a virtue that does not receive the attention it deserves. Like courage, temperance is directed to the emotions, particularly when they obstruct virtuous behavior. The second way Aquinas sees this happening is when our emotions become either so powerful that they make us rash or careless, or else so listless that we do not want to act at all. As its name suggests, temperance "tempers" our emotions either up or down. If our emotions are too strong—they may make us violent—they need to be tempered down or subdued. If they are too weak—we are depressed or lethargic—they need to be tempered up or aroused. Temperance does not silence our emotions, it channels them to the service of virtue. This virtue seeks the right balance of emotion in our actions because too little emotion hampers us by making us apathetic, but too much emotion hurts us by making us impetuous. Virtuous action depends on well-ordered affections, and this is what temperance achieves; it gives the proper expression of feeling to our actions. Thus, Thomas does not see temperance suppressing the emotions; rather, he says temperance shapes the emotions into their most appropriate expression, using them to empower virtuous behavior instead of obstructing it.

Aquinas's understanding of temperance flows from his sense of virtue. For Aquinas, virtue signifies the full liberation of human powers, never their mutilation or suppression. Virtue liberates human powers to the service of the good. The same is true with temperance. Aquinas knows human beings are creatures of powerful drives and feelings. He knows these passions can help us in doing good, but sometimes they can frustrate us in doing good. When the latter occurs, the emotions are not aids to intelligent living, but obstacles to it—they need to be refined, measured, and disciplined to the service of virtue. To speak of temperance in this way does not mean that it is "mere obedience to the cold command of reason," but that through temperance our emotions are "gradually transformed, intensified, and oriented to the goals of the person."[2] In this respect, temperance is like courage inasmuch as both virtues come into play whenever we are confronted with something that could "render us unreasonable" (*ST*, II-II, 141,2).

There are two parts to temperance: the first part is shame, the second part is honor or beauty. To speak of shame implies there is a nobility to being human beneath which we should not fall. Thomas captures this when he describes intemperance as a puerile emotion. To be intemperate is to fall beneath the true dignity of a human being. Someone who is puerile has lost control of himself, and is a slave to his emotions. His life is not well-ordered, it is reckless, chaotic, and out of control. An intemperate person is a creature of excess soon to become a creature of compulsion; when that happens, he has lost his freedom.

This is debasing. When our emotions are so misdirected that they are out of control, it is they that govern us instead of us governing them. If this occurs, our emotions become destructive, they drag us down, they shame us. Aquinas believes that certain kinds of behavior are debasing. Some things should not be done because they are repugnant to the nobility we have as creatures made in the image of God. We may not think of shame as important in the moral life, but Aquinas did. We need a sense of shame to appreciate the value and preciousness of our lives as children of God. To debase ourselves through intemperate behavior is to mock our dignity as God's loved ones, it is to "lower ourselves" in the sense that we step out of our true status as God's children and into something so much less. This is why Aquinas says, "Intemperance is shameful . . . for it debases a man and makes him dim. He grovels in pleasures well-described as slavish . . . and he sinks from his high rank" (*ST,* II-II, 142,4).

To become slaves to our emotions is to degrade ourselves. This is what Thomas means when he speaks of intemperance as a "darkening of our splendor and beauty," and as a "dulling of our true dignity" (*ST,* II-II, 142,4). It is his extraordinary respect for our nobility as humans that leads Thomas to treat intemperance as such a tragic disorder. The tragedy of intemperance is that it disfigures the beauty we have as creatures fashioned in God's image; that is why to become intemperate is to forsake our genuine dignity.

Sensitivity to shame, fear of being dishonored, uneasiness about losing our good reputation are all valuable qualities to have. To be sensitive to shame is to be anxious about possible disgrace, and this is a moral strength. We should fear disgrace, we should fear the loss of our good reputation. These are all aspects of the virtue of temperance. We need a sense of shame to alert us to the things that will debase us. Thomas captures this when he writes, "Sentiments of shame, when repeated, set up a disposition to avoid disgraceful things" (*ST,* II-II, 144,2). This sensitivity to shame, which Thomas also calls "a healthy fear of being inglorious," is an extremely valuable moral quality because it protects us from behavior that will belittle us. We know those temptations. Temptations to lose control of ourselves, temptations to surrender ceaselessly to whims and compulsions. We know how frustrating it is to lose our freedom to a compulsion, to know there is something destructive that has power over us. It is oppressive and enervating because it prevents a healthy, integrated life.

We can appreciate the importance of shame if we consider what would happen to us if we had no shame. Aquinas says shame comes from "a horror of dishonor" (*ST*, II-II, 144,4). Shame protects us from thoughtlessly risking our integrity. Shame is a sentry before all that might dishonor us. What if we lose a sense of shame? Aquinas says we can lose any feeling of shame if we have surrendered to disgraceful behavior so often that we have lost the capacity to recognize it as disgraceful. This is what is morally dangerous about giving in to intemperate actions. In itself, a single intemperate act may seem relatively harmless, but it begins a deadening of moral sensitivity, and what is most tragic is that this can happen so gradually that we are hardly aware of it. Eventually, we are numb to what is debasing about certain behavior because for us it has become a way of life; we have identified ourselves with it so closely that we cannot see it for what it is. As Aquinas explains, "Accordingly a man may lack a feeling of shame . . . because what is really shame-making is not apprehended as such, and accordingly a man sunk in sin may be quite shameless; indeed, far from being shamefaced, he may be brazen about it" (*ST*, II-II, 144,4).

The second element of temperance is honor or beauty. Aquinas argues that honorable people are virtuous people. Our honor stems not from our possessions or our power or our fame, but from our goodness. What makes us honorable is our virtue, for honor stems from moral excellence (*ST*, II-II, 145,1). Similarly, temperance is a virtue of the beautiful because it gives a proper measure or proportion to our actions, and that is what beauty is. Remember that a virtuous person is not only one who does the good, but does it in a fitting or appropriate way. For an act to be virtuous, what matters is not only what we do, but also how we do it.

This is the function of temperance. Temperance shapes all behavior into a proper balance of intelligence and passion. With temperance, every moral act is a thing of beauty; even the simplest act of kindness is something beautiful when done with style and grace. We know people whose deeds are things of beauty. They not only know how to do good, they do it with style. Their acts of thoughtfulness, their gestures of forgiveness, even the ways they surprise us display graciousness. Their deeds are works of art, perfectly sculpted acts of goodness. There is an artistry to virtue, and it comes through temperance. Far from being a virtue that chastises, temperance arranges all the parts of an action fittingly; thus, the entire act, however small, is beautiful and noble.

II. THE GIFTS OF THE SPIRIT: THE LOVE THAT BRINGS US HOME

It is not common to conclude a study of Thomistic ethics with a look at the Gifts of the Spirit, but that is how Thomas brought his study of the moral life to an end. His analysis concludes not with the virtues, but with the Gifts, and for those who have grasped well what guides and shapes his moral theology, this should be no surprise. Remember that the whole purpose of Thomas's moral theology is to reunite us with the God whose love has made us. The strategy of Thomistic ethics is to teach us how to live so that we can return to God. Everything Thomas says in his account of the moral life is governed by this concern. Convinced God is our joy, Thomas wants to show us how to live so that we can possess as deeply and intimately and lastingly as possible the love which alone will bring the peace we desire. If reunion with God is the fitting culmination of life, what must happen to us to achieve it? This is the question driving Aquinas's study of morality. It tells him what the moral life must be.

This is why he concludes his study of morality not with the virtues, but with the Gifts of the Spirit which are the virtues' perfection. Aquinas realizes that no matter how good we become, we shall never be good enough to merit God. We cannot gain God through our virtues, for before the incomparable goodness of God, our goodness, however splendid, always pales. The goal of the moral life is reunion with God, but our virtue is not capable of that because God's goodness is too far beyond our own. No matter how great our goodness, it will never be sufficient to break into the heart of God. When all is said and done, it is God's love, not our own, that brings us to God's Kingdom.

This is why the virtues find their completion in the Gifts. Our virtue is a tribute to a love we shall never equal, but can always embrace. Ultimately, Thomas knows, we return to God "in virtue" of God more than ourselves. It is God, not our virtue, that redeems us, God's goodness, not our own, that heals and restores. It is true that we return to God through love, but the return is through God's love more than our own. It is God's love which brings us home, God's love that embraces and completes our own, which is why our virtues are perfected in the Gifts of God's Spirit. The Spirit poured out in our hearts that gave us the capacity for virtue, is the Spirit through which our virtue is fulfilled.

Put differently, our love remains an invitation to God to do for us what we cannot do for ourselves, which is why even charity remains a plea for a healing, a prayer for a completion we can only receive. As a virtue, charity moves us to surrender because we know we cannot gain the Kingdom unless we allow ourselves to be brought there by God. Given the goal of the moral life, the Gifts of the Spirit are in no way superfluous; indeed, they are essential, for without the gift of God's love we shall never reach our place of belonging. As Thomas understands, it is the Spirit who takes us home.

> Thus it is written: "They that are led by the Spirit of God are sons of God and heirs"; and, "Your good Spirit will lead me into a right land." For no one can attain the inheritance of that land of the blessed unless he is moved and led by the Holy Spirit. Hence, to attain that end, it is necessary for a man to have the Gift of the Holy Spirit (*ST*, I-II, 68,2).

The Gifts of the Spirit are in no way an afterthought to Aquinas's account of the virtues, but are entailed by how he understands the virtues being rooted in love. We noted in chapter 5 that recognizing love as a passion makes every virtue a confession of need. Charity's virtues are born from a love that cries for another love to complete it. Charity's virtues are passionate for God because they recognize in God the single love that can enable them to achieve the goodness they seek. Charity's virtues always articulate need; they are cries of dependence on the love we can only receive, the perfecting, redeeming love that remains the quintessential gift.

Charity's virtues begin in passion, but they also end in passion. They are born from our passion for God, but they are completed in God's passion for us. They emerge from our passionate, supplicating love for God, but they are perfected in God's passionate love for us, a love we call Spirit, a love we know is gift. Charity's virtues take root in our desire for God, but they terminate in God's desire for us. It is God's love that takes our virtues born from charity and perfects them with the goodness necessary for reunion. On either side the virtues are bounded by passion and love, but on the far side of virtue they are bounded by a love that is purely and wholly gift.

We need the Gifts of the Spirit because our virtues, no matter how good, always fall short of the goodness of God. They can never achieve the end they intend because they intrinsically lack the goodness they need to break into the heart of God. No matter how strong or pure or vibrant, confronted with the love of God, our love is a deficiency which needs to be overcome. That virtues formed in charity find their completion in the Gifts rests on the insight that the only love capable of God is God's love. Only God has the goodness requisite for gaining God. As good as we are, we are never good enough, and that explains why we finally achieve happiness, not principally through our own activity, but through the Spirit. There is no better word than "gift" to describe this because the Gifts imply a blessing by God at exactly the point our virtues can do no more. That Thomas sees the virtues perfected in the Gifts reminds us that redemption is not a measure of our goodness, but God's.

The Relation between the Virtues and the Gifts

In Aquinas's account of the moral life, the virtues always have the Gifts in mind. Charity's virtues intend the Gifts because they know it is only in that love that they will be able to do what they are meant to do—establish Kingdom intimacy with God. Charity's virtues are gestures of love because they are formed from a passion for God; however, because they are born from this confession of need, they forever stand as an invitation to another love to bring them to completion. Remember, as Thomas told us, that in the Christian moral life we are patients and God is the healer. Every virtue formed from charity's love acknowledges the need for another love to complete it. Charity makes every virtue a homage to a love it needs but can never offer of its own.

That the virtues are perfected in the Gifts demonstrates that our virtue is exhausted at the limit of our agency. The Spirit is not something totally different from charity, but is what happens to charity at the limit of virtue. At some point in the Christian moral life our love is exhausted by the very desire from which it springs; however, that charity's love gives birth to the Spirit signals that virtue dies not in emptiness but in God. That charity ultimately breaks forth in the Spirit testifies not that we love in vain, but that our love is perfected when it is the Spirit. At the limit of virtue, charity becomes the Spirit; that is, our friendship with God is met by God's friendship for us. That virtues born from charity find their completion in the Gifts means that those who make God their love never love in vain.

It is important to appreciate that the Gifts are not something entirely different from the virtues, but are what virtues born from charity finally become. The strategy of charity-formed virtues is to become Gifts because it is only in that perfect love that they can fulfill their purpose as virtues; namely, reaching God. The Gifts of the Spirit do not replace the virtues; rather, they show what a lifetime of friendship with God does to our virtues. Charity transforms the virtues; in fact, it stretches them so completely they become something else, they become Gift. We noted that a virtue is nothing middling, but strives for our optimum possibility. Thomas realizes that the optimum possibility of every virtue—as well as our lives—is to be fired by the Spirit. Charity transforms the virtues so radically that through its love they reach another kind of goodness. The Gifts of the Spirit are virtues' most splendid possibility. They represent not another kind of virtue, but their ultimate transfiguration. The Gifts represent what charity has always sought, the full embrace of our life by God.

Thus, the Gifts are the harvest of a life of friendship with God. If grace prepares for charity, charity prepares for the Gifts. There are no Gifts where charity's virtues have not been long at work. The Gifts are not added to these virtues, they emerge from them. To have the Gifts is to be ruled by the Spirit, but the Spirit lives in us, not by chance, but because a lifetime of friendship with God has made possible the fullness of God's life within us. That is why Thomas insists the Gifts are not accidental; rather, they are intended by charity and prepared for by its love. The Gifts are formed from charity in the sense that it is the lifetime work of that love and its virtues that prepares us to receive the Spirit. Again, the Gifts are not something totally different from charity's virtues, but their most perfect expression (*ST,* I-II, 68,4).

What then distinguishes a Gift from a virtue? The Gifts are like the virtues because they, too, are habitual ways of acting that make us good, but they are different from the virtues in the agency from which they proceed. Simply put, the virtues proceed from us, but the Gifts proceed from God. We are the agents of virtue, but the Spirit is the agent of the Gifts. As Aquinas explains, "The Gifts surpass the common perfection of the virtues, not as regards the kinds of works done, but as regards the mode of operation, inasmuch as we are moved in the case of the Gifts by a higher principle" (*ST,* I-II, 68,2). That higher principle is God. To speak of God as the agent of the Gifts means that it is the Spirit who enacts these virtues within us. Thomas says there is something about the Gifts "which transcends the common meaning of virtue," and that is because with the Gifts "we are moved by God" (*ST,* I-II, 68,1). It is not God acting apart from us, but God acting within us. It is the Spirit of God fully alive in us, moving us, directing us, perfecting all our behavior. With the Gifts, God's Spirit rules our lives; God is the one by whom we are. With the Gifts, God's love is no longer something to which we tend, but the power by which we move. To be possessed by the Spirit means God's love has become the innermost principle of our lives, expressing itself perfectly in all our activity. Made one with us through charity, the Spirit dwells in us, not provisionally, but permanently, making everything we do an act of perfect praise to God.

The Fruits of the Spirit: Love, Joy, and Peace

Thomas ends his treatise on the Gifts—as well as his schema of the moral life—with a discussion of the Fruits of the Spirit: love, joy, and peace (*ST*, I-II, 70,3). The Fruits of the Spirit describe a person whose passion for God has been met. Recall that the moral life ends when peace has come to our hearts. As we saw earlier, morality is not only a matter of learning the good, but is also a matter of easing our restlessness, is a search for something so richly blessed that in possessing it we desire no more. Morality begins in the desire for wholeness, restoration and fullness of life; and it ends when the Spirit takes possession of our hearts.

When the Spirit dwells in us, we possess the most perfect and satisfying of all goods; better yet, we are possessed by it, for we are embraced by the love that has always wanted nothing more than to offer us life. To be embraced by this love is to know the Fruits of the Spirit. When we are in God and God is in us, we know the fullness of love, joy and peace. Then we love and we are loved, perfectly, flawlessly, in the everlasting intimacy of divine friendship. Then we have joy, for we are united with what we have always desired. And then we have peace, too, because the fullness of life is ours.

It is fitting that Thomas concludes his moral theology with a love satisfied and a desire fulfilled, for this is exactly what he promised. He has been a man with designs on us, a man who fervently hoped we could not journey with him and remain unchanged. Thomas wanted to share with us his vision of the moral life. It is grand and glorious, it is expansive, magnanimous, and abundantly graced. It promises the utter restoration of ourselves in love. It promises healing, wholeness, happiness and peace. The plot of the Christian moral life is to love as we have been loved. We are called to be for God who God has always been for us, a friend, a lover, one who wants to share with us all that God has. In this respect, the moral life is not so much a matter of what we do, but of what we allow ourselves to receive. God offers us the fullness of life, joy and peace; Thomas has shown us how that life, joy and peace can be ours.

If we allow God to befriend us, if we open ourselves to the love that wants nothing more than to restore and redeem, we shall know the fullness of life we have always sought and we shall find the joy and peace for which we have forever hungered. The plot of Aquinas's ethics is to enable us to be redeemed by God's friendship-love. When this happens the moral life shall be over for us, for we shall know what it means to desire no more.

9. What to Make of a God of Love? Some Conclusions about Aquinas's Vision of the Moral Life

God loves us and wants the best for us. If this is true, how must we live? It is this conviction that has driven and shaped Thomas's magnificent schema of the moral life, and this question that his reflections have attempted to answer. What are we to make of a God of perfect love? We have a God who cannot know peace until all of us share fully in that love. We have a God who is restless until the divine happiness is our own. This is why grace is relentless, ingenious, adaptable; it is also why God's love is redeeming. A God who loves each of us personally, absolutely and eternally has one abiding intention: to make sure all of us live the love, joy and peace that is God. How does an ingeniously loving God bring this to be? It is with this question that Thomas grapples as he sculpts his outline of the moral life, and this book has tried to show what he has achieved. This final chapter offers an overview of Aquinas's moral theology and a summary of our conclusions. Hopefully it will let us glimpse Thomas's magnificent vision of the Christian moral life as a whole.

Each of us born from grace is called to glory. That is the strategy of creation, that is how the universe is formed. God's desire for our wholeness is structured into our human nature; indeed, it is the innermost law of life. Sometimes we seek this glory unconsciously as we fumble for wholeness, but are not sure how it is attained, or when our restlessness leaves us searching for a peace we are not sure can be found. This is God at work in us, leading us, loving us. There is something driving us on, something persuading us not to be content until some yet to be recognized joy can be ours. This is the presence of God in our lives, the silent energy of grace. From our first stirring to life God has extended us an invitation of friendship, an offer of beatitude. The Christian moral life is the grammar of our response.

142

Actions: The Link between Needs and Their Satisfaction

We examined this first in chapter 2 when we spoke of men and women as creatures of purposes. Thomas's guiding insight is that human beings are purposeful. We act because we are seeking; we do things because there is something we are trying to achieve. To have a purpose means there is something we hope to see fulfilled. That can be a good meal, a pleasant evening, a satisfying career, but ultimately what we hope to see fulfilled is our life. Our most perduring intention is to bring ourselves to wholeness through the pursuit of something we think will complete us. Whatever this is becomes our sovereign love, and our desire for it gets expressed in everything we do. What we love most holds sway over our lives and characterizes all our behavior.

But because it is the love at work in everything we do, it is also the love that most determines who we become. This is why if we want to know what will become of us we need only look at what we most consistently intend. Our future is inscribed in our intentions. For Thomas this is our hope, but it can also be our peril if we intend something less than wholehearted devotion to God.

That we are purposeful also means we are incomplete. The reason we act is because there is something we want that we do not have. Actions are born from need. For Thomas morality begins in indigence. If we were already whole there would be no reason to act, because there would be nothing we did not have. To say that acts are purposeful is to recognize that they are the link between needs and their satisfaction. The moral life is rooted in need, it stirs in this abiding sense of insufficiency.

But what really are we after? We want a good and happy life, we want someone to love, we want enough meaningful activities to give us a sense of accomplishment. But there is something more. Embracing all these particular needs is a comprehensive and deeply personal need to find peace and abiding joy. We are not sure how to name this need or how it can be answered, but we know when it has not been met. It is the sense of incompleteness that haunts even our happiest moments; it is the emptiness that gnaws at our joy. Dimly we realize there must be some radically satisfying good, a good so fulfilling that when we have it there is nothing more we could want. Thomas called this our ultimate end, and said it is whatever we take to be our final and most perfecting good. The moral life is the quest to discover and possess this good, for we are convinced we cannot know joy until it is ours.

The Christian Moral Life: An Odyssey
Toward Happiness with God

An odyssey toward happiness is a good way to describe how Thomas sees the moral life. It begins when our desire for wholeness is stirred and it ends when it is satisfied. We talked about happiness in chapter 3, and described it as whatever can bring the full and most perfect development of ourselves. Happiness is lasting friendship with whatever is our most promising good. But oftentimes we are not sure what this might be or where it can be found. We look for happiness, but sometimes in the wrong places, not necessarily seeking something bad, but giving something more of ourselves than it deserves. This is why Thomas studied money, fame, pleasure, reputation and health as candidates for happiness. He agreed they are all good and that we need them for a flourishing life, but he concluded they could not be ultimately good because none of them alone can complete us; it is not in them that we find peace, and if we love them inordinately we are diminished.

As we saw in chapter 3, our happiness comes by cultivating a love for something so good that in being one with it we shall know incomparable joy. To be happy is to be in love with the best possible good, and for Thomas that is God. A happy person is one who lives in love with God. Lovers of God are happy because love brings likeness, and loving God makes us enough like God to find joy in God. To be happy is to hold what we love in our hearts and to let that love change us. It is in our assimilation to God that we find happiness, in our union with God that we find joy.

A God who wants what is best for us wants us to share the divine happiness as deeply as possible. Recognizing this led Thomas to describe our happiness as charity, and to speak of charity as friendship with God. We looked at this in chapter 4 and found Thomas working to capture exactly what our relationship with God must be if we are to know full happiness. We have a God who squanders nothing, a God of such extravagant generosity that everything in the divine life is ours. How then must we be related to God so that God's happiness can be ours? Thomas answered that we must cultivate for God the kind of friendship-love God has always had for us. We looked at the three marks of friendship and considered what they meant. We spoke first of benevolence. To be benevolent toward a friend is to seek what is genuinely good for the friend. Part of the life of every friendship is to be devoted tᵣ one another's good. If we are speaking of charity-friendship with God, it means watching after the interests of God, acting on behalf of the plans and purposes of God, and in all things striving to make things better for God.

But benevolence is not enough for friendship. Mutuality is the second characteristic of friendship, and it reminds us that friendships exist only where affection and care are reciprocal. This mutual exchange of the good that forms the friendship makes friendship important for the moral life, because it is in and through the life of good friendships—what Aristotle called friendships of virtue or character—that we come to know the good, delight in it, and grow in virtue. Applied to God, Thomas spoke of charity as a "certain society" in love that we have with God. An exchange of love and goodness takes place in our friendship with God, and as with every friendship it changes, forms, and shapes us. This is why we can speak of charity as lifelong conversion to the goodness of God. Through the love given and received in friendship with God, we slowly take on the goodness of God.

Doing so brings us likeness to God, a likeness sufficient to enable us to see God as "another self," which is the third mark of friendship. This is how good friends think of one another. Their friends are so important to them that they cannot imagine themselves without them. They know if they change their friends they change their self, this is why a friend is "another self" to them. The same holds true in our friendship with God. To speak of God as another self is to realize we cannot be ourself without God, but it also means there is a way God cannot be God without us. That is the measure of love; an acknowledgment of mutual need and mutual enrichment. Friends bring life and delight to one another, and the same holds true in our friendship with God. This third element of friendship reminds us that our self is our friendship with God and it is in this relationship that we will grow to fullness.

Love: The Cornerstone of Thomistic Ethics

If we come to fullness through friendship with God, then learning to love rightly is the most crucial challenge of the moral life. What becomes of us turns on what we love and how we love, which is why we need a love that will make us both happy and good. We considered this in chapter 5 when we began our discussion of the role of the passions and emotions in the moral life, especially the primacy of love. In following Thomas's analysis, we noted that the energy of the moral life is rooted in us as creatures of appetites. We reach out to something we perceive as good, but something we also lack and want for our completion. Morality stirs from this awareness that there is something we need but lack; thus, we reach out to possess it. Here begins the process of love, for we love whatever good we think will bring us wholeness, and realize it is a good we cannot offer ourselves but can only receive.

But why do we reach out at all? Thomas says it is because we have experienced its goodness and felt its value. We move through life with open hearts. The world is rich in blessings and we feel them. We love something only because we have felt the touch of its goodness. We reach out to make something our own because its value and beauty have broken through to us, not peripherally but essentially; we have been marked by its loveliness.

This is what led Thomas to call love a passion. To love something is to have suffered its goodness; it is to have felt, been moved, and even changed by its loveliness. The moral life turns on this ongoing dynamic of being touched and responding. Thomas's account of the passion of love taught us that human beings are made to receive something: the goodness of the world, the preciousness of another person, the everlasting beauty of God.

We stand in absolute need. This is what Thomas's analysis of love teaches us. We live in need of a completion we can only receive, and it is through love that we receive it. Love signals our openness to life and captures our availability to everything good. That we are made to love means we can be made whole, but it also means we must cultivate openness and receptivity to all the things that can truly enrich us. Creatures of absolute need, we must also be creatures of abiding hospitality. We sense this when we feel deeply our need to love and be loved by another. To love another is to receive them fully into our lives and let their love remake us from within. It is the love of another that heals us and frees us for life. The rehabilitation of our self through love is a project of the moral life for Thomas, and it happens when we make ourselves available to those who can bring us a wholeness we could never offer ourselves. This is why we could speak of charity as abiding openness for God, and say that one of the express strategies of charity is to make us supple before the God who redeems, heals and gives life.

We examined the emotions in more detail in chapter 6. Thomas distinguishes two groups of emotions, the affective or concupiscible, and the spirited or irascible. The first plots the movement of the moral life from love through desire to joy. But we focused more on the second group of emotions because we recognized their importance in helping us continue the journey to God. It is true that morality begins in love, works through desire, and is completed in joy, but life seldom works so felicitously. Sometimes we are tempted to give up our quest for the good because we tire of it. We grow weary of trying to be good, and may even grow bored with the virtuous life. Other times we are discouraged because there is much that thwarts our best intentions, whether it be bad luck, misfortune, or evils that overwhelm. The spirited emotions strengthen us to be resolute in our pursuit of the good. They help us persevere amidst hardship or adversity.

In our reflections on the spirited emotions we gave special attention to hope because we know oftentimes it is hope that cradles love unto joy. But we also reflected on what it would mean to lose hope. To become hopeless is to no longer believe anything great is possible for us. In Aquinas's schema of the moral life, that is disastrous for it is to deprive ourselves of the unsurpassed good God wants to be ours. Thomas envisions stunning possibilities of life, wholeness and love for us, but we must believe in them and hope for them. To lose hope is to close ourselves off to what is most promising. We are called to live with great expectations, and hope enables us to sustain them. To believe in anything less than our grandest possibility is to deny that what God wants for us can be ours. In a sometimes difficult life, hope helps us strive for the best we can be. It is an indispensable ally, for it insists that we be who God wants us to be. Put differently, if God wants what is best for us, hope enables us to want the same.

The Virtues and the Gifts: Habits That Bring Us Likeness to God

But glory is not automatically had. It is the work of a lifetime, our work as well as God's. From our side, glory describes the radical transformation of the self through the virtues. Aquinas has an ethic of virtue because he knows the reunion of ourself with God turns on the transfiguration of ourself in godliness. Happiness is lasting intimacy with God, but it is a kinship possible only when we are enough like God in goodness to have union with God. This is what the virtues help achieve, the ongoing, penetrating remaking of ourself through habits that make us godly. We need to develop the virtues because godliness does not come naturally to us, nor does it come easily. The virtues respect the awesome potential we have to achieve something noble and beautiful with our lives, but they also recognize that our promise can be destroyed and our goodness can be corrupted. Poised between possibilities for greatness and depravity, our lives are ours to make. We make them good through the virtues, but vices destroy us.

We reflected on this in chapter 7. We spoke of the virtues as characteristic ways of acting that make both the action and the person good. Virtues are transformative activities because by developing good habits the quality of a good act becomes a quality of a good person. Virtues characterize us in goodness, whether that be the goodness of justice, forgiveness, patience, generosity or compassion. A virtuous person is not one who does the good sporadically, but one who does it predictably, delightfully, and with a certain ease. These persons are at home with doing good because they have become good themselves. The great consolation of the virtues is that they promise we can become better. The virtues are means of moral development, and there is nothing piddling about the goodness of which they say we are capable. The virtues reach for our ultimate potential, and if they are charity's virtues they reach for the holiness of God. Virtues formed in charity measure moral development in terms of God's goodness, which is why there is no limit to what they strive to achieve and no point at which their work is finished.

It is also why the virtues become the Gifts. The work of a virtue is measured by the goodness it is given to achieve. If the goal of virtue is a human or natural goodness, we can meet such goodness on our own. But it is not that way with charity's virtues. Virtues born from charity seek the supernatural goodness of God. With grace we can reach for that goodness, but we can never master it. This is why any study of Aquinas's account of the virtues is incomplete if it does not recognize that charity's virtues are perfected in the Gifts of the Spirit.

This is what we saw in chapter 8. We learned there why for Aquinas the moral life both begins and ends in gift. It commences with the outpouring of grace in our hearts, which enables us to do good in the first place; but it is also the gift of God's Spirit that completes what our goodness could never achieve. Our virtue is perfected in the Gifts of the Spirit because only God can offer us the goodness we need to enjoy perfect, everlasting friendship with God. A God of perfect love wants what is best for us, but only a God of such stunning goodness can make it possible for us. Our radical need is never overcome. From first to last we depend on God to offer us what we cannot give ourselves. God seeks perfect friendship with us, but only God can make this possible.

This is the work of the Gifts of the Spirit. They achieve that final sanctification that enables Kingdom-friendship with God because when the virtues become the Gifts, the Spirit is the innermost principle of our lives. God is fully alive in us, befriending us with a love that heals, restores and redeems. When the Spirit dwells freely within us, God is able to love and bless us in exactly the way God has always desired. This is divine friendship, the Spirit fully alive in us, God's grace delightfully at play.

What are we to make of a God who loves us and wants the best for us? This is the question Aquinas's moral theology has tried to answer. Yes, there has been a strategy to his outline of the moral life. Thomas wants us to surrender to the love that has always loved us. He wants us to succumb to, not resist, the chorus of the universe. It is and has always been a chorus of love, an untiring song of care from a God whose love fashions all things and cradles them to fullness. To appreciate this and to respond to it is the goal of Aquinas's moral theology. He wants us to open our hearts to the gift of love that will make us whole. He wants us to say yes to it, to embrace it, to delight in it. Our lives are to be a dwelling for God, our hearts a center for God's friendship. If we suffer such openness to God we shall know love, joy and peace. These are the harvest of the Spirit at play in our lives, and these are what our hearts have always secretly sought. Love, joy and peace—it is for them we have hungered, for them we have so tirelessly longed. Thomas shows how the deepest hungers of life are satisfied: our hearts find rest in God.

It is a rest born from a love we never deserve and can never equal. It is peace flowing from a love that shines through everything and pleads for our acceptance. The strategy of the Christian moral life is to make us the kind of people who can say yes to perfect love. That such love exists testifies that everything is gift. That such love can be ours testifies why to know God is to worship God. Perhaps this is why Thomas Aquinas said that to sing praise and glory to God is the best thing we can do, our most perfect moral act. Perhaps it is why all that he wrote and achieved seemed in the end as mere straw compared to the glory that belongs to us all. More than anything, perhaps it is why for him the moral life ends in silence and awe.

Notes

1. Meeting a Man with Designs on Us

1. James A. Weisheipl, *Friar Thomas D'Aquino*. Washington, D.C.: The Catholic University of America Press, 1983, pp. 3–6.
2. Weisheipl, p. 10.
3. Josef Pieper, *Guide to Thomas Aquinas*. Notre Dame: University of Notre Dame Press, 1987, p. 11.
4. Weisheipl, p. 17.
5. Weisheipl, p. 17.
6. Pieper, p. 18.
7. Weisheipl, p. 19.
8. Weisheipl, p. 30.
9. Pieper, pp. 124–125.
10. Pieper, p. 12.
11. Weisheipl, p. 44.
12. Weisheipl, p. 45.
13. Pieper, p. 89.
14. Pieper, p. 93.
15. Pieper, p. 93.
16. Pieper, p. 93.
17. Pieper, p. 95.
18. Pieper, p. 95.
19. Pieper, p. 22.
20. Pieper, p. 96.
21. Pieper, p. 96.
22. Pieper, p. 94.
23. Weisheipl, p. 241.
24. Pieper, p. 15.
25. Weisheipl, p. 243.
26. Weisheipl, p. 236.
27. Weisheipl, p. 301.
28. Weisheipl, pp. 319–320.
29. Weisheipl, p. 320.

30. Weisheipl, p. 321.
31. Weisheipl, p. 322.
32. Weisheipl, p. 322.
33. Weisheipl, p. 324.
34. Pieper, p. 17.
35. Pieper, p. 101.
36. Weisheipl, pp. 220–221.
37. Pieper, p. 115.
38. Pieper, p. 115.
39. Pieper, pp. 79–80.
40. Pieper, p. 84.
41. Pieper, pp. 85–86.
42. Pieper, p. 87.
43. Pieper, p. 82.
44. Pieper, p. 82.
45. Pieper, pp. 83–84.
46. Pieper, p. 100.
47. Pieper, p. 77.
48. Pieper, p. 83.
49. Pieper, p. 99.
50. Pieper, p. 159.
51. Pieper, p. 160.

2. Why We Do Anything at All: A Look at Human Behavior

1. *ST,* I-II, 1,1. All references to the *Summa Theologiae* are taken from the Blackfriars/McGraw-Hill edition, New York: McGraw-Hill Book Co., 1969. Subsequent citations from the *Summa* will be incorporated in the text.
2. Paul L. Holmer, *Making Christian Sense.* Philadelphia: The Westminster Press, 1984, pp. 29–30.
3. John Finnis, *Fundamentals of Ethics.* Washington: Georgetown University Press, 1983, p. 139.
4. Finnis, p. 139.
5. Finnis, p. 140.

3. Happiness: The One Thing Everybody Wants

1. Jean Mouroux, *The Meaning of Man.* Garden City, New York: Image Books, 1961, p. 24. I am grateful to Fred Sucher, C.P., for bringing Mouroux's works to my attention.
2. Mouroux, p. 25.
3. Mouroux, p. 25.
4. Mouroux, p. 22.

5. Mouroux, p. 26.

6. Mouroux, p. 16.

7. An excellent analysis of this theme can be found in Robert Johann, S.J., *The Meaning of Love*. Glen Rock, New Jersey: Paulist Press, 1966.

4.   Charity: The Virtue of Friendship with God

1. Etty Hillesum, *An Interrupted Life*. New York: Washington Square Press, 1981, pp. 186–187.

2. Robert O. Johann, *The Meaning of Love,* pp. 46–47.

3. Lynne Sharon Schwartz, *Rough Strife*. New York: Harper & Row, Publishers, 1980, pp. 17–18. I am grateful to Mary Liekweg for bringing this book to my attention.

4. Aquinas, *Scriptum Super Sententiis Magistri Petri Lombardi*. Paris: P. Lethielleux, 1933, III, d. 27, q. 2, a.1.

5. Aquinas, *Scriptum Super Sententiis Magistri Petri Lombardi,* III, d. 27, q.2, a.1.

6. Aquinas, *Summa Contra Gentiles*. Book Three, Part I, tr. Vernon J. Bourke. Notre Dame: University of Notre Dame Press, 1975, 3, c. 19.

7. See Joseph Keller, "De Virtute Caritatis ut Amicitia Quadam Divina," *Xenia Thomistica Theologica,* II (1925), p. 256.

8. Jean Mouroux, *The Christian Experience,* tr. George Lamb. New York: Sheed and Ward, 1954, pp. 263–264.

5.   The Passions and Affections in the Moral Life:
Exploring the Primacy of Love

1. See Jean Mouroux, *The Christian Experience,* pp. 237–238.

2. For a fascinating, insightful discussion of love as the basic force of all life, see Brian Swimme, *The Universe Is A Green Dragon*. Santa Fe: Bear & Company, 1984, pp. 43–52.

6.   The Passions and Affections in the Moral Life:
Finding the Strength to Go On

1. Josef Pieper, *On Hope*. Translated by Sr. Mary Frances McCarthy, S.N.D. San Francisco: Ignatius Press, 1986, p. 21.

2. Pieper, p. 28.

3. Pieper, pp. 54–56.

4. Pieper, p. 57.

7. The Virtues: Actions that Guide Us to Fullness of Life

1. Enda McDonagh, *Between Chaos and New Creation.* Wilmington, Delaware: Michael Glazier, Inc., pp. 1–9.

8. The Virtues: Finding our Perfection in a Gift

1. On this point see Stanley Hauerwas, "The Virtues and Our Communities," *A Community of Character.* Notre Dame: University of Notre Dame Press, 1981, p. 123.

2. Andre Guindon, *The Sexual Language: An Essay in Moral Theology.* Ottawa: The University of Ottawa Press, 1977, p. 64.

Index